DATE DUE

AY   2 2011

America Through the Eyes of China and India

America Through the Eyes of China and India

Television, Identity, and Intercultural Communication in a Changing World

Edward D. Sherman

continuum

NEW YORK • LONDON

2010

The Continuum International Publishing Group Inc
80 Maiden Lane, New York, NY 10038

The Continuum International Publishing Group Ltd
The Tower Building, 11 York Road, London SE1 7NX

www.continuumbooks.com

Copyright © 2010 by Edward D. Sherman

Library of Congress Cataloging-in-Publication Data
Sherman, Edward D.
America through the eyes of China and India: television, identity, and
intercultural communication in a changing world / Edward D. Sherman.
    p. cm.
Includes bibliographical references and index.
ISBN-13: 978-0-8264-2270-5 (hardcover : alk. paper)
ISBN-10: 0-8264-2270-5 (hardcover : alk. paper)
ISBN-13: 978-0-8264-3092-2 (pbk. : alk. paper)
ISBN-10: 0-8264-3092-9 (pbk. : alk. paper) 1. Television broadcasting–
Social aspects–China. 2. Television broadcasting–Social aspects–India.
3. Television programs–United States–Influence. 4. China–Civilization–
American influences. 5. India–Civilization–American influences.
6. Intercultural communication–China. 7. Intercultural communication–India.
8. Intercultural communication–United States. I. Title.

PN1992.3.C6S42 2010
384.55–dc22   2009054103

ISBN: 978-0-8264-2270-5 (hardback)
       978-0-8264-3092-2 (paperback)

Typeset by Newgen Imaging Systems Pvt Ltd, Chennai, India
Printed and bound in the United States of America by Thomson-Shore, Inc

For Sarah

Contents

Introduction

Scene #1: India

The temperature outside is hovering somewhere between standing in a blast furnace and walking on the surface of mercury. I have long since sweat through my own clothes and have actually begun to sweat through the clothes of those around me as if by some strange process of glandular osmosis. If the intense temperatures are not enough to push me to the point of delirium, there is a cacophonous symphony of car horns so loud and persistent that if they stop for even a moment my ears ring from the silence. The very air I breathe is filled with a bouquet of aromas that somehow manages to be ethereal, tempting, and nauseas at the same time (try to imagine the smell of floral incense, fried food, and urine, as though you were standing in a port-a potty next to a fried dough stand in the middle of a mountain meadow). My eyes, burning from the sweat and partially blinded by the sun, attend to a man, walking past a Reebok store and a Pizza Hut wearing saffron robes and carrying a walking stick and a begging bowl. All the while, I have been being followed for the past 20 minutes by a woman who keeps repeating, "chapatti, chapatti, chapatti for baby." I am unsure whether she wants a chapatti to feed her baby, wants to trade a chapatti for her baby, or is asking me whether I am willing to trade my baby for a chapatti. Since I have no baby, no desire for someone else's baby, or any spare bread, I decide not to respond.

As I continue on my path, I pass by a small temple wedged between a Nescafe coffee stand and someone offering fresh fruit juice that is made in a blender that appears to have not been cleaned since 1987, maybe 88. I begin to make my way over to the juice stand, choosing to ignore the threat of dysentery for the sake of hydration, but become enveloped by a sea of men chanting and jumping up and down in front of the temple deities. After having been showered with water, having flames waved in front of my face, and having my forehead marked by some type of red dye that I am fairly sure is causing an allergic reaction, I finally extricate myself from the crowds and continue toward the juice but not before being stopped by someone asking, "Which country?" After initially thinking that I would answer that I do not much like country music, but realizing that my shining wit would likely not be appreciated, I replied "USA." The reply came quickly, "Ah, USA very good country." Hearing this, my mind flashed to rising unemployment, a shaky economy, gun violence, racial inequality, a faltering educational system, Britney Spears, crumbling infrastructure, pollution, Wal-Mart, government corruption, Paris Hilton, secret CIA prisons, and Texas. Not wanting to get into a prolonged discussion, and still severely dehydrated, I just smiled, wobbled my head, and turned toward the juice stand. Just as I was about to order, the power goes out keeping the biohazard blender from either quenching my thirst or infecting me with microbes, amoebas, worms, viruses, or parasites—a fair trade.

Feeling somewhere between exhausted and unconscious I decide to return to the relative comfort of my hotel room to enjoy the air conditioning, which while effective sounds something like a cross between a lawnmower going over a rock garden and a smoker with a chest cold, but then when you spend 9 dollars a night on a hotel the fact that there is even a bed is fairly exciting. Being simultaneously tired, overstimulated, dehydrated, confused, hungry, and just shy of mentally unsound, I decide that all I can do is watch TV. Leaning back against a headboard that looks as though it is out of a Bollywood movie, I hit the power button and watch the TV flicker on. After a few minutes, and various commercials for whitening cream, fatafat snack food (can't even make that up), and Nike shoes advertised by playing cricket on the top of a bus, something familiar appears before my eyes. The image on the screen is a source of comfort and security in a foreign land, a sense of warmth and familiarity, and a reminder of the great society to which I belong, *Desperate Housewives.*

This is a book about television, which is to say that it is a book about culture, communication, and who we are. Which we? Americans of course. What other nationality in the world could possibly deserve an entire book to be written about them. Other nations may deserve a few pages perhaps, maybe a magazine article or a pamphlet, but certainly not an entire book. For example, France: croissants, wine, cigarettes, labor strikes, and the impressive ability to be defeated in every battle. Or perhaps Australia: kangaroos, boomerangs, penal colony, aborigines, and Crocodile Dundee. America, on the other hand, cannot be summed up in a few lines; we are an impressive people; we are a people to be emulated, simulated, and respecterated (borrowed that one from George Bush). If the American people were not admired around the world, and the American identity was not one that everyone desires to take on, why would American television programming be as popular as it is. I am sure there can be no other possible explanation than the fact that we are loved around the world and that all of those polls showing negative views of America around the world standing at 49%, only 5% lower than Iran, must be mistaken or produced by those angry liberals at CNN.

In this book we will examine the interrelation between television, identity, and intercultural communication in a global world, through a careful consideration of China and India. China and India are specifically chosen because they have my two favorite types of food and writing this book gave me an excuse to travel to both countries. As much I enjoy a good dosa and mu shoo (perhaps I have thing for pancakes), food is secondary to the fact that China and India are now collectively home to one-third of the world's population, have two of the fastest growing economies and militaries in the world, and are reshaping the very idea of geopolitical power and national alliances. To ignore these two countries is, as the expression goes, to ignore the elephant, or in this case elephant and dragon, in the middle of the room.

The sheer size, rapid development, and good food of India and China (well, at least India) are not the only reasons to include them in this study. Perhaps more important, to properly understand the dynamic interaction between television, identity, and intercultural communication, an examination of cultures that are wholly other from that of the land of NASCAR and Kentucky Fried Chicken is desirable for both theoretical and rhetorical reasons. In truth it would be hard to find cultures that were more completely wholly other than China and India. In the one we have a nation with thousands of years of history; a cultural landscape made up of the combination of Buddhist, Taoist, and Confucian ideas; a government that is simultaneously Communist and state capitalist and has a tendency towards state control, oppression; and accusing the Dalai Lama for earthquakes (oddly, all these things seem to go together). In the other is also a nation with thousands of years of distinct cultural history, but in this case influenced by a religion of 10,000 gods (9000 just wasn't enough), Muslim and British rule, and the legacy of Gandhi and Nehru. To walk the streets of either nation is recognize the vast cultural differences and to find yourself face to face with the wholly and at times holy other. One example of the holy other is seeing a group of people whose cheeks are pierced with long metal spears dancing around with ceramic pots with burning fires on their heads in 120 degree heat, while my religious upbringing included falling asleep in a nicely pressed suit as a man droned on about something to do with burning bushes, plagues, wandering in a desert, and a golden cafeteria (I think that I may have misheard the last part because I was always hungry by the end of services).

While this book will focus on China and India the theory and analysis put forward speaks to a much larger range of considerations. The rapid, pervasive, and continual interaction between people of distinct cultures, histories, backgrounds, religions, and ethnicities that exists within our global world, and which, short of an act of Shiva playing in his role of destroyer or Jesus sounding the trumpets of the rapture (Pat Robertson can hope), will continue to increase guarantees that issues of identity and communication will stand at the forefront of concern and consideration. For better or worse (better when it is Jeopardy worse when it is Celebrity Family Feud) television occupies a central place in the interaction between diverse groups both within and between cultures. American television programming whether viewed via satellite, as is the case in India, or pirated off the Internet or on DVD, as is the case with China, carries the images of the American nation, people, and identity in all of its complexity, from the narcissistic bliss of American Idol to the paranoia-inducing, time-traveling fun of *Lost*.

But even as these images are broadcast around the world; what we do not know is how they are received. The images themselves may not change, the little yellow id that is Bart Simpson looks like Bart Simpson no matter whether the image is broadcast in the United States or Djibouti (by far the best name of any country), but how it is received, perceived, and understood can differ infinitely. If, for example, the same image of former president George Bush is broadcast into a Republican and Democratic household, what is actually seen is distinct. In the first instance, it is an image of a messenger of god, a modern-day knight Templar fighting the evil infidels and protecting the American Holy Land from falling into the hands of heathens. To the other household, the image is a picture of Satan, that is, if any of them were to actually believe in hell (but of course they would be far too educated and progressive as to accept such a childish concept spawned by such a trivial thing as religion). We have only one image, but there are two distinct, and in this case diametrically opposed, understandings of the image. The fact that people understand things differently is rather obvious and in no way limited to televised images; just think of any conversation you have ever had with your spouse or significant other— you may think you are talking about the same thing but you quickly realize that it is as if you are living in different worlds (I hope that's not just me).

The issue of what is displayed or articulated and how different people receive it is particularly exigent in terms of identity and communication. How we understand ourselves as Americans (brilliant, virtuous, just, god-fearing, defenders of democracy, freedom, and Twinkies) and how we are understood by others (obese, oafish, moralizing, irascible, gun slingers) can be at significant variance. Similarly how we as Americans understand others can be at significant variance with their self-understanding. This was made abundantly clear to me when I was trying to teach a lesson about East Asia and asked my students to tell me what they thought about when I said the word *China*. Their replies, which I could not have made up even if I tried (as creative as I am), included such things as slanted eyes, Chinese food, fortune cookies, Communism and Hello Kitty (this last one showing that Japan and China are clearly interchangeable). What we have here are two sets of people, each with their own self-understanding and being understood otherwise by the other group, and in turn misunderstanding the other group. Just in case you are not yet confused, add in the fact that cultures themselves are not internally consistent, leading to considerable variance of self- and other-understanding within a culture or nation as well, and you have the formula for a situation that will either require Excedrin, Prozac, or maybe just a stiff drink.

With all of this identity confusion, communication across cultures becomes deeply problematic. Trying to understand what someone means when we do not recognize how she or he views her or himself or how that is influenced by the cultural world in which she or he resides is like trying to play scrabble using Hebrew tiles when you speak Telugu (unless of course if you are one of the four Jews in Andhra Pradesh, India). This is to say that the possibility for meaningful communication across cultures is directly tied to issues of identity. To carry this one step further, to the extent that television programming is a significant source of cultural images, particularly of Americans, those lucky enough to have access to American programming will begin to develop a sense of the American identity. This sense of what it is to be American will be at variance with how Americans view themselves and contributes to a situation in which meaningful conversation becomes more difficult than getting Jerry Falwell to go to a gay club. This difficulty is not insurmountable (unlike the Jerry Falwell issue), and one task of this book will be to explore how we can use confusion to lead to understanding—as much sense as that makes.

The first chapter of the book will examine issues of identity and culture in a global world. Both of these terms become particularly problematic in the contemporary age and have been argued over more frequently than whether it is acceptable to wear white after Labor Day. Since I am never the one to pass by the opportunity to kick a dead horse, I will engage this topic and try to present a position that can serve as a basis for our discussion of media and communication. We will move toward a position in which both identity and culture become unproblematic through a phenomenological (it is great fun to use big words) shift that privileges the lived experience of identity and culture over the countless theories about them. To put this another way, it is one thing to read a cookbook, while it is another to bake a cake. Academic discourse has for too long put theoria before praxis (also great fun to use non-English words) and in doing so has taken something obvious and made it complex. Or as one colleague of mine once put it, we are like a bunch of geniuses staring at a lollipop.

Chapter 2 will build upon the basis of culture and identity laid out in Chapter 1 and draw out its implications for media studies. As engaged actors (which is better than married actors since most Hollywood marriages end in divorce), we are not simple receptors of cultural information. We are always actively interpreting what we receive through our self-understanding that is directly tied to our cultural metaphors. If we are to understand the meaning of the images we view, we need to tend to both our personal reactions (i.e., falling off the couch laughing at the contestants on American Idol, wishing that I had every pair of shoes in Carrie's closet—a bit odd since I am not a woman—or getting frustrated when the evidence just does not add up in CSI) and the cultural world that informs our reactions. What we will come to see is that the intended meaning of the show, or the culture in which it is produced, matter far less than how it is received. It is sort of like buying new clothes: It does not matter how they were made or where they were made, what matters is how it fits in with your personal fashion sense, and what is in style at the time.

In the second section of the book, Chapters 3 through 6, we will turn from the theoretical groundwork (I just imagine a whole group of highway workers staring at a road asking, "Well, how do we know this road even exists?" and another replying, "It was the Buddha who once said that there is no difference between the object and the observer.") to examine the specific cases of China and India. Chapters 3 and 5 will outline the media markets in China and India, respectively, providing a basic sense of how the market is structured along with significant trends and developments. Chapters 4 and 6 will take specific examples of popular television programs and employ the work from Chapters 1 and 2 in an analysis of these programs by putting each on a couch and asking it about its earliest childhood memories—or maybe just a critical analysis. Through this we will both illustrate (crayons and paper sold separately) the issues of identity, culture, and media discussed earlier in the book and offer insight into the cultures, identities, and self-understanding of those living within China and India.

Having deconstructed the ideas of identity and culture, as well as the media images portrayed in China and India, we will begin to put the pieces back together in Chapter 7 and unlike Humpty Dumpty they may actually go back together again. Specifically, we will look at the multi-vocal nature of media images in cross-cultural contexts, and how multiple cultural metaphors can be placed upon the same representation. From this we will begin to see a very different picture of the American identity that does not include the arrant narcissism of American Idol, the cheaply perfumed desperation of the *Bachelor*, the Dionysian drive for pleasure in *Sex in the City*, or the intense existential anxiety of *Lost* that would make Jean Paul Sartre look like Dr. Seuss. Rather than our vision of ourselves in all of its glory and decrepitude we find something in-between, a third as it were, which is neither quite American, Indian, or Chinese; it is Ameridian, or Indirican, or Amerinese, or Chinerican, or, well you get the idea.

The final chapter of the book will explore how the type of identity, cultural confusion, and reinterpretation that is continually present in a global world may actually be able to serve as a basis for meaningful intercultural communication. To even understand that we misunderstand one another demands that we share a tremendous amount in common. We may interpret what we encounter differently, but if we understand how and why this misunderstanding occurs we learn invaluable information about both ourselves and the person with whom we are interacting. In a sense, what we want to do is become like Socrates, or the Buddha, and recognize that all that we know is that we know nothing (easy enough for me). If we recognize that we begin with a fundamental misunderstanding, we can begin to work toward a form of meaningful intercultural communication.

One final note. Since the American government has suggested that people need to be more active, and we know that government is never wrong, I have provided exercises at the beginning of some of the chapters. While these exercises may provide more mental activity than physical, albeit you may have to pick up a remote that could require you to walk across the room, the goal will be to get you to engage in the kinds of practices that inform this work. This is to say that issues of identity, culture, media, and communication are ones that we encounter in our daily lives and of which we all have first-hand experience. Using these experiences will help to make the remarks contained within these pages seem more like a friendly conversation over a cup of coffee, in front a fire place, on a cold winter day, with the snow falling, and Christmas music playing in the background, and visions of sugar plums dancing in your head, or at least more personally meaningful.

Stay tuned, there is more fun and excitement after this short commercial break.

1

Globalization, Culture, and Identity: Oh My!

Exercise #1

Put down this book (after you finish reading the directions) and go look in a mirror. The first thing I want you to do is try to answer the question, "Who am I?" If this seems too large of a task, since I would not want you to get overwhelmed at such an early point in the book, try listing some of the things that make you who you are. Do this part first.

(Imagine elevator music playing in the background)

Now that you have your answer or list, look at the type of words you use and what they describe. Did your descriptions operate on the level of doing or being? If, for example, you wanted to mention something about your occupation did you say, "I am a student," or "I go to school"? Did your list describe your physical appearance, emotions, feelings, thoughts, dreams, desires, or a combination of these things? Take a minute and review your list, and notice what you included and, perhaps more importantly, what you left out.

(More elevator music)

Some of you may have included your national, ethnic, or cultural background as part of your list, elements that are often so close at hand that we do not notice them (it is like someone asking you what color shirt you are wearing—as obvious as it would seem, you probably need to look down to check). Take a minute now and write down a description of your cultural or national background. Do not be a C student and simply list the places, shoot for the A+ and offer an actual description of your culture or national identity.

(More elevator music—but a new song)

Once again, I want you to attend to the types of things you chose to include. Does your list refer to specific symbols such as flags, crosses, stars, or golden arches? What about specific ritual practices, like setting off explosives to celebrate the birth of your country, eating the body and blood of the Son of God, or circumambulating (a word you do not get to use very often) a large black cube. Or maybe you referred to the personal characteristics like the brave and strong Americans, the hot-blooded passionate Italians, the precise and industrious Germans, or the Canadian Canadians (you try to come up with something for Canada—and I lived there for five years). After having thought through how you described your cultural background, compare it to your description of yourself and try to notice if there is a connection.

(Back to the first song)

The importance of this exercise is that for the most part, in our everyday lives, we do not think about our cultures and identities—they are unproblematic. When you compared your list about yourself to your list about your culture did you find an overlap or influence? Are you defined by cultural characteristics, practices, symbols, or ideas? Are you a red blooded, flag waving, believer in life, liberty, and the pursuit of happiness—at least for other people like you? Or do you feel separate or alienated from your culture, like a democrat in rural Mississippi? As you move through the first chapter keep all of these questions, as well as your answers, in mind.

There is a direct, intimate, and inexorable connection between identity and culture. Whether we like it or not (and at this moment everyone reading this book in a blue state is shaking their heads in dismay) who we have been, are, and will become is only possible within and in relation to a particular cultural horizon. To extend this claim further, all acts of human understanding from speech acts to abstract thought are possible because of and are made sense of in terms of a cultural world. The cultural mediation of understanding extends through self-understanding as well, or to be even more radical we are each an embodied expression of the cultural world in which we find ourselves.

We do not learn a culture; we are our own particular history and culture. For those who are fans of migraine inducing, impenetrable German philosophy, Heidegger once expressed a similar idea when he noted that we are thrown into a world not of our own making.[1]

Since there is a good chance that at least a few readers are sitting with their brows furrowed and mouths open wondering how I can assert such things without any form of argument or proof, the majority of this chapter will be used to work out these claims through a careful consideration of issues of culture and identity in a global world. The first step in achieving this end is to start at the beginning (a very good place to begin—thank you *Sound of Music*). As the opening exercise in this chapter hopefully demonstrated the first thing we need to do is to, as Wittgenstein claimed was the entire task of philosophy or in this case media studies, clarify the words that we use.[2]

The words we need to clarify are the very ones that this chapter is about: global, culture, and identity. We, for the most part, use these words in rather nonproblematic sort of way, the same fashion in which we use most language. If you were to say, "I want a banana," you would probably not trouble over what it means to want something, if wanting is the same as desiring, if the Buddha is right about desire leading to suffering, if by wanting the banana you are walking down a path of rebirth and suffering, or if to want in this case is more an expression of your enjoyment of bananas and not your desire for them. The majority of the language we use is employed in fairly limited and conventional sense, and it could not be otherwise. As various linguistic theorists have pointed out, to be able to say anything at all demands a tremendous amount of agreement and understanding between those communicating.[3]

While the conventional use of words in which we do not think about their meanings is probably beneficial for everyday conversation (could you imagine trying to order at McDonald's if you had to get into a prolonged discussion about the nature of food and whether what they are serving even qualifies), it is not sufficient for a consideration of subjects such as identity and culture. While these words can be used in an unproblematic way, they are the expression of an abstraction, something that is simultaneously present in the world and yet impossible for us to directly identify. If I were to say point to a table we could all point to something assuming that there is a table in the room. If I were to ask you whether you have an identity, most people, assuming no severe psychological malady, or a degree in philosophy (which may be one in the same), would answer yes. Yet if I were to ask you to point to that identity, you may vaguely gesture toward yourself (or offer another gesture toward me that involves only one finger). What I am suggesting is that while we can sit and discuss about the tableness of a table, as fun as it may be, it is for the most part unnecessary. If, however, we are going to discuss such things as identity, culture, globalization, words that do not refer to easily objectifiable things, a clarification of terms is inherently necessary. We will begin with globalization.

We Are the World

Globalization is one of those fun words that comes into common parlance and is bandied about by scholars, pundits, conservatives, liberals, and every other talking head to such a degree that we might actually believe that either they actually know what they are talking about or are at least talking about the same thing. The fact that words come into vogue is itself curious; it is as though they are the new hip club that everyone just has to get into. As someone who has taught courses in history and religion, I have often struggled with the currency of this term, since in its most basic form it means little more than the world being interconnected. As anyone who remembers high school history would know (admittedly very few do since it tends to induce sleep faster than Benadryl), there has never been a point in human civilization in which there has not been significant global interaction. A wonderful example of this is the South Indian port city of Cochin in which you can find Dutch churches, Chinese fishing nets, and ancient synagogues, sitting next to temples for Siva and Vishnu. If globalization is nothing more than the interaction of peoples and cultures than it is certainly nothing new, or particularly confusing. But of course it must be more complicated than that.

In contemporary usage the term *globalization* can refer to anything from the interrelation of economies to the undue influence of a certain unnamed, but rather obvious since it is the only one, superpower of the world. Interestingly, a recent poll by the BBC found that more people believed that globalization (particularly American influence) is a greater threat to the world than terrorism—a finding that is somehow simultaneously startling and not at all surprising (it makes me feel all warm and fuzzy to be an American).[4] Economists, political theorists, anthropologists, sociologists, and pretty much any other group that ends in an -ist or -ism applies this term readily to suit their particular needs or ends. It is clear that the specter of this thing called globalization is very much present in our world, but what it means, or would mean to live in such a world is far less clear.

Since the Ghostbusters will likely be of little use in tracking down the specter of globalization (wow, that was bad even for me), a better approach may be to examine a few perspectives to see whether we can arrive at some degree of commonality. Thomas Friedman, in his work *The Lexus and the Olive Tree*, asserts that globalization is " . . . the inexorable integration of markets, nation-states and technologies to a degree never witnessed before—in a way that is enabling individuals, corporations and nation-states to reach around the world faster, deeper and cheaper than ever before."[5] From Friedman's perspective, globalization is not something new (apparently he stayed awake in high school history), but it is faster and more pervasive than ever before. Common to many theories of globalization, Friedman seems to be suggesting that everyone has near immediate access to the broader world.

Perhaps Friedman has seen things that I have not, but I am fairly well sure that villagers in rural India, China, various African countries, large parts of Southeast Asia, as well as Central and South America, are not on the Internet, watching satellite television, reading the *New York Times*, or spending hours everyday on Facebook "friending" people (a term that I find somewhat troubling being that most of my "friends" know less about me than the clerk at the local convenience store) from other countries. Their lives may be affected by the impact of the decisions of their governments in terms of global trade or alliances, but these are fairly far removed from the average person's daily life. I am well aware that the United States participates in something called the North American Free Trade Agreement (NAFTA); I know that it has something to do with taxes on imports and exports, and I also know that I am suppose to like it, hate it, feel the need to fix it, destroy it, and yell about it depending upon my political persuasion (which I think at this moment is the Bull Moose Party). As a concerned American citizen with a good education, I dutifully engage in high-minded debates about the merits of free trade, arguing rhetorical loops around my opponents mainly because I do not know what I am talking about. Even with all of my immediate access to the global media and economy I cannot say as that I have felt the effect of NAFTA, but then I also have never felt the effect of NATO, the UN, Kyoto Protocol, the G8, the G4, the World Bank, the IMF, or the CIA—well, there was just the one time. The point here is that there is a vast gap, chasm, canyon, rift, gorge, or sinkhole between theories about the effects of globalization and how it is actually experienced.

Anthony Giddens, one time director of the London School of Economics and personal advisor to Tony Blair (which apparently did not work out so well), wrote that globalization " . . . is best understood as expressing fundamental aspects of time–space distanciation. Globalization concerns the intersection of presence and absence, the interlacing of social events and social relationships "at distance" with local contextualities."[6] We will pause here momentarily so that everyone can scratch their head and reread the definition. Translated from Academic to English, he is basically saying that globalization is the interaction between what is right in front of us, and what we cannot see. For example if I go into Filene's Basement to buy Calvin Klein undershirts (I happen to like Calvin Klein . . . at a discount) I am directly encountering the cheap price and indirectly benefiting from unseen child labor, sweat shops, and government oppression thousands of miles away. This "distanced" interaction goes on all the time, even though for the most part we remain consciously unaware of the indirect aspects, which is a good thing since as comfortable as they are, I am unsure whether I could buy the undershirts if I had to buy them directly from a sweat shop.

Giddens' idea of globalization is interesting in the sense that it is fairly broad and allows for the inclusion of a wide range of phenomena. It helps us to see that anything from NAFTA to renting Bollywood movies (something that if you have not done provides an excellent opportunity to work on your choreographed dancing), can be seen as aspects of globalization. However, the problem is that the same reason that makes it interesting is also why it is not particularly useful. If almost everything in the modern world can be seen as globalization, then nothing is globalization. It is sort of like having a common denominator in a math problem; you can divide through and have the equation left unchanged (my seventh-grade math teacher would be very proud). The other issue with Giddens' definition is that it is unclear to what extent globalization as "dinstanciation" is actually experienced by an average person. Much like with Friedman, Giddens assumes that his theory actually matches with some form of lived experience, a rather common disorder among those who have spent too much time in the academy. As my previous example of buying undershirts shows, I may be participating in what Giddens views as a globalized world, but I am experiencing it as though it is just my normal, average, everyday, daily, quotidian, banal, prosaic, predictable existence.

One more example will be particularly useful as we move forward through the book. Jan Aart Schlote in her work, *Globalization: A Critical Introduction*, suggests that there are five different possible understandings of globalization: internationalization, liberalization, universalization, Westernization, and deterritorialization (bigwordinization and makestuffupinization did not make the list).[7] Of these, Westernization is the one that people most often associate with globalization particularly in a negative light. More specifically, it is the omnipresent Golden Arches, shining their bright light of freedom upon people dressed head to toe in Nike and Reebok clothing, while drinking a bottle of coke, listening to Mariah Carey, and watching stuff blow up in big summer blockbuster movies, which makes people fearful of the undue influence of American culture around the world. The concern is that, in some way, traditional cultures, ways of being, and values are endangered by the presence of corrupting external influence. An interesting assumption among people who hold this view is these cultures are somehow "better" and deserve or need to be protected.

The globalization as Americanization perspective is the one not only most commonly recognized but it is also the one most often fought against. Those people who conceive of globalization in this way often take a normative stance in denouncing its negative effects on the populations of other countries. The odd irony of course is that the very people who antiglobalization activists want to protect are the ones most drawn to American culture, at least in its popular forms. This position assumes a rather paternalistic perspective (us White folks have to protect them Brown folks from us White folks). It is like a father telling a child what is good for them and what they should or should not do, except in this case its academics and pundits telling the common folk they are making a mistake. The problem here is the same as it was for Giddens and Friedman; when theory becomes detached from lived experience, all kinds of zany things can occur. The vast majority of the 6.3 billion (probably 7 billion by the time this book is printed) people inhabiting this world do not worry about the meaning or implications of globalization in the course of their everyday lives; they simply encounter the world in which they live. Parts of the world are more integrated than they ever have been in history, but not all parts. Many of our actions in our immediate physical location are connected to or affect distant unseen places and people, but we tend not to recognize it. And American culture is widely consumed abroad, but it is not clear that this is necessarily a problem. In truth, globalization refers to such a broad range of phenomena that it becomes like modern art, interesting to look at but open to infinite interpretations. Rather than standing around scratching our heads while staring at a giant mobile made out of tin cans (my wife is an artist so I have gotten quite good at seeming interested—"Ah, yes, that really does provided a fasci- nating commentary on modern consumption and the US industrial blah blah blah . . . "), we can look to globalization in another way.

Globalization can best be understood as the lived experience of people in the contemporary world relative to their geographical, cultural, and economic position. The word *contemporary* is chosen care- fully (unlike most of the others that I just randomly put on the page), because globalization is not about modernity, or high, late, or postmo- dernity. The world we inhabit is and has always been global; what changes is the form. For some, globalization will be the experience of finding work at a factory in China because an American manufacturer has decided to outsource labor. For someone else, it might be the ability to buy cheaply made products at Wal-Mart, while for someone else it could be the experience of going online and learning about the diverse tribes of Papua New Guinea (one of my personal favorite pastimes). The phe- nomena are clearly not the same, yet each one can be recognized as globalization. What this points to is that globalization is not a thing or even coherent; it is the experience of people living in one world together as the nature of this togetherness continues to unfold in new, interesting, confusing, dumbfounding, amusing, bemusing, unsettling, encouraging, and largely incomprehensible ways. The consideration of globalization shows us that what we need to do is attend to the lived lives and dynamics of the people and events we wish to understand, something that seems as obvious as the fact that Texas is a scary place to live, but that is often overlooked. In other words, to do service to a study about the interaction between media, identity, and communication with regard to America, China, and India, we cannot look at it as just another example of globalization, because there is no such thing as just another example. Nor can we turn toward it as the representation of something else, since everything is only what it is in itself even if it looks similar to something else (i.e., it is fairly easy to confuse one sorority girl with another, but believe it or not if you look closely enough they are actually different—slightly different shades of blonde hair). If we are to understand the relationship between media, identity, and communication, we must start with the particular and move toward the general. To attain this end, we must next turn our attention to something that is often considered one of the major sources of particularity and difference (no, not fashion) culture.

Getting Cultured

There are few words that are more widely used and misused, few ideas more vaguely defined, and few human phenomena more difficult to pin down than culture. Culture is one of those interesting things that fits into the category once provided by Supreme Court Justice Stewart Potter in a discussion of pornography when he said, "I cannot define it, but I know it if I see it." To utter the word *culture* is to evoke images of everything from Beethoven to Busta Rhymes, from Rembrandt to Andy Warhol, and from baseball and apple pie to cricket and chat (not idle conversation, but the oh-so-delicious Indian street food that simultaneously offers the opportunity for gastronomic delight and gastrointestinal distress). The word *culture* has been used to refer to everything from cultural products such as art and music to the entire breadth of human civilization. Due to this promiscuity of usage (we are all linguistically licentious at times), it is difficult to clarify this term and demonstrate its relationship to identity and communication, but it is a task we at least need to try to undertake. As always, the best place to start is at the very beginning (I may have watched the *Sound of Music* one too many times as a kid). One of the first definitions of culture put forward was by Edward Tylor in 1871 in his work *Primitive Culture*, in which he views it as " . . . that complex whole which includes knowledge, belief, art, law, morals, custom, and any other capabilities and habits acquired by man as a member of society."[8] The sense of culture that Tylor provides is very much in line with the sort of everyday notion that we usually employ in casual conversation: Why did you go to the museum? To get a little culture. Why do you use a knife and fork? Just part of my culture. Why do you drive a car designed for military use that only gets 6 miles per gallon, while going to the warehouse store to buy 14 pound boxes of Cheerios even though you only have one child? Its part of good old American culture. In terms of common parlance Tylor's definition certainly covers our conventional understanding of culture, but in this it is also limited and not particularly enlightening.

There are two interesting issues raised from Tylors position: one about the location of culture, and the other about the boundaries of culture. He claims that culture is something that is "acquired by man as a member of society," as if it was sort of a like getting a driver's license and as long as you can read the eye chart and parallel park you will get it (which a shocking number of people are not able to do). The implication of this claim is that there is some point at which the individual stands prior to culture as some type of empty vessel waiting and needing to be filled up. This strange idea of the person as the tabula rasa is deeply tied into Enlightenment thought and a type of Western ontology that privileges the individual over the collective, the one over the many, becoming over being, self over other, and dogs over cats (perhaps not the last). In this vision of the human person we are born free and independent and can learn a culture, subject ourselves to collective rule, and choose to join into social forms. What I have always found particularly fascinating about this idea is that I personally cannot recall a time in which I either did not have a cultural world or in which I agreed to consent to collective social life. It is not as though as a 6-month-old I was carefully collecting and acquiring cultural fragments like an anthropologist taking notes on an indigenous tribe in New Guinea ("Ah yes, and here we observe the patriarch of the family employing some type of sharp tool to remove the meat from the carcass of the dead bird while the matriarch seems to be informing him that everything he is doing is incorrect. Personal note: I am tired of subsisting on strained peas and I need my diaper changed"). While this may be an exaggeration (of sorts) the point is clear, culture is not something outside of us that we acquire, it is something that we live and embody.

Anyone who has traveled realizes that where one region ends and other begins is not always clear. For example, what counts as the American South? Few would deny that Alabama and Mississippi are Southern states and yet southern Florida would not be included on most lists while northern Florida would (unless my map skills have gotten particularly bad or there has been significant tectonic activity, south Florida is South of all of the others). In the sense used, the *South* refers more to a cultural milieu than it does to an actual geographical location, but even *Southern* culture varies from one location to the next. This is to say that if you are in Nashville you may be enjoying country music and Biscuits from the Loveless Café (Oh so delicious), while in New Orleans it may be zydeco and gumbo (also delicious). The very idea that a culture is "whole" is difficult to accept, because anything that tends to be placed under this label, whether it is art, customs, or Broadway shows, tends to be fluid and dynamic and open to multiple influences and interpretations. Where Southern culture ends and mid-western culture begins is not clear—St. Louis and Kansas City both have barbeque but the charmin' Southern drawl has gone missing. A culture is like a cloud; it is permeable, it can move, it can change form, and yet something remains that we can recognize.

Much like the definitions of globalization we considered, this initial definition of culture seems to forget the same important thing: There is a division between theory and practice. Culture is not simply an object of study; it is the lived experience of human beings in this world from the simple act of eating a McDonald's hamburger, to riding an elephant to a wedding—something that I did not get to do even though I got married in India (a very long story that might deserve its own book or maybe a made for TV movie). Culture is not something objectively experienced by the person living it; it is deeply value laden. Max Weber made this point in his work on methodology. For Weber,

> The concept of culture is a value concept. Empirical reality becomes culture to us because and in so far as we relate it to value ideas. It includes those segments and only those segments of reality which have become significant to us because of this value reference.[9]

Another way of looking at this is that a tree would not be part of culture unless we care about it, and if we care about it then it is part of culture. The reasoning here may be more circuitous than a line at Disney World (the best place on Earth, but one which my wife will not allow me to go until we have children—maybe I can borrow someone else's), but the point is an interesting one: There are certain objects or experiences in the world that are subjective or value laden while others are not. Or to put this another way, culture does not touch everything and everything is not culture.

The idea that there is a sharp division between the objective and subjective, between the neutral and value laden, and between rationality and belief has been roundly challenged by many thinkers involved in fields of methodology and philosophy of science (a somewhat ironic title yes, but one that few in the field find particularly amusing—academics don't have the best sense of humor).[10] The idea put forward and one common to considerable amounts of postmodern thought (another ironic title) is that we encounter every object, subject, or phenomenon through a particular lens, meaning that there is never actually a neutral or objective position. If you and I were both sitting on an interstate in traffic I may be encountering a dehumanizing experience of being trapped in a small metal box among thousands of other people trapped in small metal boxes, while you may be feeling a sense of excitement that you have an excuse not to go out with your in-laws for dinner (certainly not an experience I have ever had). If there is no neutral encounter of the world, than all things are value laden. Viewed from this perspective, Weber's idea that certain things stand outside of culture becomes problematic because there is no objective thing that value-laden human experience does not touch.

Weber moves us in the right direction when he suggests that we should pay heed to the evaluative aspect of culture, but again does not remember the most obvious thing: For the most part, we live our lives and do not reflect on them (we are Americans after all). When I stand in front of the American flag I do not ponder the meaning of the value of freedom and liberty; I just get a sense of pride (this may be somewhat untrue—I was actually repeatedly thrown out of my high school home-room for not saying the flag salute). This nonreflective encounter with the world shows how much our culture is in and through us. Culture is not something that we acquire; it is not something that has firm bound-aries or limitations, nor is it something we actively contemplate on an everyday basis. Rather, culture is something we are, something we live, and something we express.

The sense of culture not as something that is optional but rather something directly tied into the human experience of the world can be well expressed through the metaphor of language. The German philoso-pher Wittgenstein, as nutty as he was (and he was nutty even by academic standards; he actually stopped doing philosophy to become a kinder-garten teacher and built his sister a house the was a plain perfect rectangle), provides a fascinating lens through which to consider culture. Wittgenstein asserts that to know a language is to know a form of life.[11] What he means by this cryptic line is that is that language is not a simple correspondence between words and images, but the expression of a particular way of being in the world. For example, were I to say the words Burger King in present day America, most people would think of a fine dining establishment that is home to the Whopper. If, however, I were to get into my time machine, zip off to medieval Europe and utter the same words (assuming I was not burned at the stake as a witch for getting out of a time machine) people would think that I was referring to some city official that became the king.

Wittgenstein, at another point claims, "The limits of my language are the limits of my world."[12] While again a bit vague (something Ludwig was particularly good at being), the meaning is that for each of us the world is coextensive with our ability to express our world. If we encoun-ter something particularly strange or novel in the world, lets say a hippopotamus wearing a track suit jumping on a trampoline while reciting verses from the Quran (I have an odd imagination), we would likely think that it is some type of performance piece, a joke, or one too many drinks. It is not that we could not understand this phenomenon in terms of itself; it is that we would initially and for the most part draw upon the language we already have available to us to describe or express what we have seen. In this, our language is the limit of our world, but it is a limit than can be moved and altered over time (unlike the speed limit, which I like to think I can alter but often find the police disagreeing with me). Languages grow and change over time, adding new words to adapt to the changes in the world. Not only that but each language user employs a different lexicon, so that even if they are drawing from the same language, the linguistic elements used will likely be different. Both Sarah Palin and I speak English, but I would like to think that my command of the language is somewhat different (perhaps better) than hers.

For the sake of this book we will view culture like a language. It is something that is primarily experienced in a nonreflexive way, structures our encounter with the world, and is simultaneously shared and open to limitless variety, creativity, and personal interpretation. Our culture is coextensive with our encounter of the world but is always open to change and reformation. This is to say that, as one of our foremost newscasters Steven Colbert once put it, I am America, and yet that America that I am will not be identical to the America that you are. I may be the liberal, highly educated, social conscious, tree-hugging, Birkenstock-wearing, granola-eating blue-state American, while you may be the gun-toting, beer-drinking, football-watching, SUV-driving, axis-of-evil-hating, red-state American, but the Americanness remains. Or to once again borrow from our friend Ludwig, there are overlaps, webs of connection, and family resemblances.

The Oracle at Delphi (Think About It You'll Get It)

Up until this point we have been like a plane landing in the New York area, slowly circling the runway trying not to run out of gas (I hate flying). The seat-belt sign has just gone off, and you can feel free to move about the cabin since we have reached our final destination: identity. As I said at the beginning of this chapter, there is a direct and inexorable connection between culture and identity. Who we are, how we understand ourselves is not only a phenomenon mediated by a cultural lens, but is actually the embodied expression of a culture filtered through our own lives and experiences. In a sense what I am suggesting is that to properly understand the connection between media, identity, and communication, we need to take a somewhat unconventional look at these topics (in case you have yet to notice I enjoy the unconventional), and be willing to question some of our basic assumptions about individuality, freedom, and choice (also known as the holy trinity of Western culture).

The debate over the meaning of identity has occupied a central place in Western thought since the late nineteenth century. Certainly questions of identity existed before this time, but the idea that identity is a problem is something novel to the past 100 to 150 years (lucky us). In truth, however, much of the confusion about identity has come about as the result of asking the wrong kinds of question, or as Heidegger once noted, the question contains the answer. If we ask why identity is a problem, why it is breaking down, or what kind of effects globalization and media will have on the self, we are assuming that it is a problem, it is breaking down, and there will be specific effects. It is sort of like when someone turns to their child and says, "How much do you love mommy?" The child may be sitting there thinking I sort of wish this woman would leave me alone or get me some ice cream but will likely reply, "very much." The only thing discovered through this interaction is that the mother thinks the child should love her, and nothing about the actual quality of the child's love (sorry to disappoint anyone). Identity is assumed to be unstable and uncertain in the contemporary age, and when we find examples of it being this way, we have proven ourselves right. While this reasoning is near infallible, sort of like when I ask my students why they think something and they reply because I do, it is not terribly helpful.

An interesting example of this assumption of fragmentation comes from the sociologist Zygmunt Bauman (of whose first name I am deeply envious). Bauman suggests that in the current age, which he labels "liquid modern" (which I guess if you were heat to a high enough temperature becomes gaseous modern), " . . . the world around us is sliced into poorly coordinated fragments while our individual lives are cut into a succession of ill-connected episodes."[13] He goes on to say,

"To be wholly or in part out of place everywhere, not to be anywhere ... may be an upsetting, sometimes annoying experience."[14] Bauman paints a picture of the modern world and identity as being fragmented, disjointed, and always out of place (it is as though the entire world has become those awkward middle school years we all wish we could forget—I have long since burned all of the pictures). The idea that we are always out of place is fascinating and yet deeply problematic. Similar to what we said for globalization, if we are always out of place, then we are never out of place, since it is the everyday experience of our identity. The out-of-place-ness becomes matter-of-fact-ness (go on, make up some of your own words, its good fun), when it is always there. In this sense it is part of who we are, and not necessarily something we experience as a problem. If you were to go from job to job, city to city, house to house, sea to shining sea, you would not experience this as an identity crisis; you would still live and encounter yourself as yourself.

Part of the problem that leads to the confusion over identity is a divide between two ways of using the term: On the one side, we have sameness or strict identity, while on the other we have similarity.[15] Strict identity is the idea that something remains exactly the same across time. Philosophically speaking this idea is deeply problematic, but then what idea is not problematic for philosophy (I actually once spent an entire 3-hour seminar discussing the meaning of the word "is" at which point I decided that this "is" a reason to switch to another discipline). In the most basic sense we can think of strict identity in terms of an object, in that the computer I am using to write this will be the same computer 10 minutes from now, 4 hours from now, or 5 years from now (though it will be completely obsolete—darn you Steve Jobs). The other sense of identity as similarity, means something more to the effect that, even though there may be changes over time and some differences, we can still recognize something as what it is. If, for example, I was to go get a haircut and then went to my parents house for dinner, it is unlikely that they would think some stranger was trying to break into their house and call the police (albeit my mother is a very nervous woman, so I suppose it could happen).

Identity as sameness is seldom if ever something that we can apply to human beings or cultures, since they are dynamic, complex phenomena that change and develop over time. Few people would say that they are exactly like they were when they were three years old (although apple juice and graham crackers do sound good), and yet short of a significant mental disorder, no one would say that they are not the same person. The problem of identity tends to arise when people assume that some sense of strict identity or sameness should be able to apply to the human person, and forget that fluidity, change, and development are not so much problems as they are aspects of human being. In fact, the same thing can be said about cultures. Much of the fear and concern about globalization (globaliphobia, or maybe occidentaphobia, or perhaps Americaphobia, or better yet McPhobia) comes from the assumption that cultures should remain constant over time, even though there has never been a point at which they were. The constancy of identity is directly tied to its relationship to culture, not through the stability of culture, but rather through its ability to adapt and change.

George Herbert Mead was one of the first to recognize the powerful connection between identity and the broader culture. He held that if we want to understand the individual person, we must begin with the whole and work back toward the individual, since it is only in terms of the whole that we can understand the part.[16] In some sense this seems rather obvious, but in a society that values individualism to the extent that we do this point gets lost more easily than Jessica Simpson in a library. We come to be in a cultural world and because of this who we are is made sense of in terms of this cultural world. Even the outsider who feels as though she may not fit within a given culture, feels this experience of disconnect and alienation in relation to that culture. Mead actually carries this point one step further when he suggests, "It is the social process itself that is responsible for the appearance of the self; it is not there as a self apart from this type of experience."[17] Our identity is not an objectified thing that exists in itself; it is a fluid process that unfolds in relationship to our social and cultural world.

To claim that our identities exist only in relation to a cultural world is not to deny that we are engaged individual actors capable of making rational decisions (in truth many of us are not hence the prevalence of giant SUV's, warehouse stores, Chihuahuas, shorts with writing on the bum, signs that inform you that you cannot brings weapons on a plane, girls with the name Mackenzie, and Texas). Culture may be directly tied into who we are, but it does not mean that we cannot reflect on it or call it into question. Mead, drawing upon the work of William James, separates our identity into two parts, the "I" and the "me." "The 'I' is the response of the [person] to the attitudes of others; the 'me' is the organized set of attitudes of others which one himself assumes."[18] Our identity as a person is simultaneously made up of our cultural world, which is always in flux, and our ability to think about, cogitate, reflect upon, respond, and react to the cultural dynamic. Or to return to a previous metaphor, we are America, but we can also realize that we are America. The interplay between our embodiment of culture and our ability to critically engage culture and ourselves will be central to a proper understand of the relationship between television, identity, and communication.

Identity, like globalization and culture, is best understood through its lived experience and less through some abstract theory or notion. We for the most part do not think of ourselves as fragmented or whole, continuous or discontinuous, liquid or solid, or in terms of any other category that theorists create for the sake of study. In what is going to be the most obvious line of this entire study, we just are. When I go to Starbucks to buy my triple shot, half caf, vente, no milk, no whip, no sugar, no coffee, latte, I am clearly not thinking about my identity; I am buying a cup of coffee (or at least some form of hot beverage). If I am walking down the street listening to one of the 37,148 songs that I have on my ipod, while texting my friend, and looking up directions on my iphone/blackberry/android phone, I am too busy walking into to telephones poles to reflect on the meaning of my being, who I am, or the state of my identity. And, if I sit down in front my 87-inch flat-screen HD TV hooked up to HD digital cable, an HD recorder, and an HD DVD player, to warm myself in its comforting glow I am probably not contemplating the effects of globalization on my culture and myself (just the $17,856 credit card bill that I have to pay off). What I am doing in all of these instances is living my identity and experiencing the world through this identity, not worrying about its meaning or status.

In terms of cultural and media studies, identity can best be understood as our individual lived embodiment of our cultural world in its dynamic complexity, and our ability to reflect upon and adapt to this world. While for the most part our identity is something lived and experienced in a fairly uncritical way, we have the capacity to step back from the everyday experience of ourselves and reflect upon both our individual identity and the culture from which it arises (even if there are a good number of us who choose not to use this ability). Identity, like culture, is something that continues to change and develop over our life course in relation to the conditions of the world. Try to imagine a professional cheerleader on a desert island refusing to give up or adjust her identity to fit the cultural and physical reality ("Give me an F, give me an I, give me an R, give me an E, and what does that spell? Fire"). While few of our lives will encounter such extreme and odd examples as this, all of our identities are constantly undergoing change. The dynamic quality of identity is essential to our ability to understand the contact between cultures, a point that we will return to in later chapters.

We are now in a position to end this chapter where we began (I like circles). Think back to the opening exercise; I know it was a whole chapter ago now so I will give you a few minutes. Your initial description of yourself likely did not include such things as inhabitant of an interconnected global world, or the complex dynamics of your culture, because as we noted these are things we tend to live and not necessarily reflect upon (don't go back and change your answers now—that would be cheating). The fact we experience our culture and identity as directly interlinked and residing within a world in which globalization is always present in a multitude of complex ways presents us with an interesting picture of ourselves as simultaneously expressing and innovating our world. This picture, which would look something like Da Vinci and Jackson Pollack working together on the Mona Lisa, or perhaps Andy Warhol collaborating with Michelangelo on the Sistine Chapel (Jesus and Campbell's soup, mmm . . . mmm good), allows us to think of ourselves in terms of our experience and the phenomenon of being human, rather than beginning with an abstract theory and placing it upon ourselves or our subject of study.

The idea of beginning with experience rather than theory, something that will be particularly important in the chapters to come, allows us to look and see what is happening when we watch American programming, and when those from China or India see the same images. The approach of turning first to encounter and experience will help to clarify the issue of who we are, who they are, who they see us as being, who we see them as being, who we see them as seeing us as being, who they see us as seeing them as being, who the they see us as seeing them as seeing us as seeing them as being (now isn't that much clearer). In the end, how we experience our identity in its relation to culture and the world directly affects how we encounter media and, in turn, how we understand others and engage in acts of intercultural communication. But I would not want to give everything away in the first chapter. Don't touch that dial, we'll be right back.

Notes

1. Heidegger, Martin. *Being and Time: A Translation of Sein and Zeit.* State University of New York Press, 1996.

2. Wittgenstein, Ludwig, G. E. M. Anscombe, and Elizabeth Anscombe. Philosophical Investigations: The German Text, with a Revised English Translation 50th Anniversary Commemorative Edition. 3rd ed. Wiley-Blackwell, 1991.

3. Morton, Michael. The Critical Turn: Studies in Kant, Herder, Wittgenstein, and Contemporary Theory. Wayne State University Press, 1993.

4. "Globalisation 'bigger threat than terror.'" *BBC*, April 9, 2004, sec. UK. http://news.bbc.co.uk/2/hi/uk_news/3613217.stm.

5. Friedman, Thomas L. The Lexus and the Olive Tree: Understanding Globalization. 1st ed. Anchor, 2000, p. 7.

6. Giddens, Anthony. *Modernity and Self-Identity: Self and Society in the Late Modern Age.* 1st ed. Stanford University Press, 1991, p. 21.

7. Scholte, Jan Aart. *Globalization: A Critical Introduction.* Palgrave Macmillan, 2000, p. 16.

8. Tylor, Edward Burnett. *Primitive Culture.* New York: Harper, 1958, p.1.

9. Oakes, Guy. "On the Unity of Max Weber's Methodology." *International Journal of Politics, Culture, and Society* 12, no. 2 (December 1, 1998): 293–306.

10. See Kuhn, Feyerband, etc.

11. Wittgenstein, Ludwig, G. E. M. Anscombe, and Elizabeth Anscombe. Philosophical Investigations: The German Text, with a Revised English Translation 50th Anniversary Commemorative Edition. 3rd ed. Wiley-Blackwell, 1991, p. 75.

12. Wittgenstein, Ludwig. *Tractatus Logico Philosophicus.* 2nd ed. Routledge, 2001.

13. Bauman, Zygmunt. Identity: Conversations With Benedetto Vecchi. Polity, 2004, p.12.

14. Ibid, p. 13.

15. Ricoeur, Paul. *Oneself as Another.* University Of Chicago Press, 1995, p. 116.

16. Mead, George Herbert. Mind, Self, and Society: From the Standpoint of a Social Behaviorist. University Of Chicago Press, 1967, p. 7.

17. Ibid, p. 142.
18. Ibid, p. 175.

Suggestions for Further Reading

Allen, Douglas, and Ashok Malhotra. *Culture and Self: Philosophical and Religious Perspectives, East and West.* Westview Press, 1997.

Bauman, Zygmunt. *Identity: Conversations With Benedetto Vecchi.* Polity, 2004.

Friedman, Thomas L. *The Lexus and the Olive Tree: Understanding Globalization.* 1st ed. Anchor, 2000.

Giddens, Anthony. *Modernity and Self-Identity: Self and Society in the Late Modern Age.* 1st ed. Stanford University Press, 1991.

Heidegger, Martin. *Being and Time: A Translation of Sein and Zeit.* State University of New York Press, 1996.

Mead, George Herbert. *Mind, Self, and Society: From the Standpoint of a Social Behaviorist.* University Of Chicago Press, 1967.

Morton, Michael. *The Critical Turn: Studies in Kant, Herder, Wittgenstein, and Contemporary Theory.* Wayne State University Press, 1993.

Nancy, Jean-Luc. *Being Singular Plural.* 1st ed. Stanford University Press, 2000.

Ricoeur, Paul. *Oneself as Another.* University Of Chicago Press, 1995.

Robertson, Roland. *Globalization: Social Theory and Global Culture.* Sage Publications Ltd, 1992.

Scholte, Jan Aart. *Globalization: A Critical Introduction.* Palgrave Macmillan, 2000.

Wittgenstein, Ludwig, G. E. M. Anscombe, and Elizabeth Anscombe. *Philosophical Investigations: The German Text, with a Revised English Translation.* 50th Anniversary Commemorative Edition. 3rd ed. Wiley-Blackwell, 1991.

2

Watching TV Is Good for You

Exercise #2

Go turn on your television. For once in your life no one will be able to fault you for watching too much TV. In fact, you get to tell people that you are watching TV for scholarly purposes, that they just do not understand how significant of a cultural medium that it is and that all of those hours spent watching *Lost* were actually a form of research (few people will actually believe this, but it does sound good).

Now that your television is on pick a program—anything from a game show (I always enjoy the *Price Is Right*; where else can knowing the price of soup win you a car) to a soap opera (no preference here, albeit I did enjoy when the *Days of Our Lives* meandered into the realm of the occult). Here comes the difficult part of this exercise: watch the program. Juts sit there and watch whatever it is you chose for 10 to 15 minutes and write down anything that may strike you, any observations, reactions, comments, concerns, grocery lists, or anything else that may come to mind as you watch the show.

(I turned off the elevator music for this exercise so it would not interrupt your viewing pleasure.)

Put your television on mute for a minute and look at your list (don't worry, the showcase showdown won't start till the end of the show). What did you notice and what type of remarks did you write down? Did you attend to the set, lighting, and production quality? Did you notice the political and economic messages being put forward by the programs, like the *Price Is Right* being a defender of the virtues of

31

capitalism? Did you notice how you feel as you watch these programs, such as an odd feeling of nausea and discomfort as you realize that Shakespeare would turn over in his grave if he could see the melodrama of soap operas? Or did you pick out particular encoded cultural messages, subversive ideas, and subtle misrepresentations, like the treatment of men on *The View*?

Next, turn the sound back on (if you haven't already) and begin to watch the same program again, but this time spend 10 to 15 minutes watching for things that can fit into the following categories: economics, gender, race, politics, technology, and religion. Watch carefully, because while not every program may contain something in each of these categories, many of them will if you attend closely to what you are watching. Look for representations, language, or ideas expressed by the program that fit into each of these categories. For example, if you are watching *Oprah* you may notice the prophetic nature of her speech and her use of money to buy the loyalty and devotion of her audience (not that I have anything against *Oprah*).

(No elevator music, just me tapping my fingers waiting for you to finish.)

Okay, now turn off the TV (Just turn it off, you can watch more later for research purposes of course). Look at the list you made this time and compare it to your previous list. Do they look similar? Did you attend to the same kinds of things, or did having a specific list change not only what you watched for but also how you watched? Were you more active in your watching (relatively speaking of course, since really unless you were sleeping, you probably could not do less physical activity, and if you sleep walk it might actually be more). Did your encounter of the program change? What about its meaning or purpose?

Giving you a list of categories is sort of like those books you use to get when you were a child that just had you run a wet brush over the page to have the picture emerge, which is incidentally still my level of artistic ability. If you approach the study of television, or for that matter any media form, with a pregiven theory, what you will come out with in the end is information to fit that theory. The point of this exercise is to show that it is important to look and see what is there and not impose a preexisting category upon it, something that will be explored, explained, cogitated, reiterated, but hopefully nor regurgitated, throughout this chapter.

Watch What You Are Doing

In the last chapter we worked through the interrelationship between culture and identity in a global world, arriving at a picture in which identity and culture are intimately connected and continuously dynamic. This picture of identity and culture, which, due to its shifting and dynamic nature, looks more like a drawing on an etch-a-sketch than a classical painting, serves as the groundwork for the subsequent sections on media and communication. The reason we began this way is that far too often people writing about media and communications come up with theories that are not grounded in any well-formed concept of the person. It would be like designing a chair that requires our knees to bend in the other direction, making a car that is too small for a person to drive, or electing a president who does not know how to govern (although we Americans have a particular knack for this last one). If you do not have a sense of what you are trying to understand or accomplish, it is terribly unlikely that you will have much success (or perhaps you would, but you just would not know it, since you do not know what you are looking for).

We cannot very well discuss television without having a sense of the viewer, nor can we discuss communication without an understanding of those doing the communicating, and yet too often this most obvious of points is overlooked. This is to say, that rather than imposing a theory about media or communications onto people, we should begin with the people to arrive at the theory. It is sort of like cooking dinner: You do not decide that you want pad thai and then look in your fridge to find that you only have a bottle of ketchup, four-day-old Indian take out, and something that was probably once a loaf of bread but now more closely resembles a small furry animal. Rather, you look in the fridge to see what you have and work from there (in this case, you are likely going out to eat). To properly understand media and intercultural communication we should begin with a specific anthropology, or understanding of the human person, and work from there. If, for example, we were to conceive of humanity as easily manipulated, gullible, and uneducated (a.k.a fans of *Rush Limbaugh*), our theory of media may focus on issues of power and domination, which has in fact been a fairly common view. The position taken in this book is, however, perhaps a bit more positive or at least less despairing.

We will approach the study of media in general, and television in particular, not through a certain theory be it Marxist, neo-Marxist, structuralist, poststucturalist, postmodern, decosntructionist, or feminist (I have often wondered, because I clearly have too much time on my hands, that if I went so far post something that I could possibly end up back where it began). Since I have a fear of commitment, rather than aligning ourselves with any school or movement we will instead try something a little bit different, not quite Michael-Jackson-different (RIP), but different. What we will attempt to do is to look and see what the relationship is between television and viewers, how we actually encounter and interact with the TV (I like to take mine out to dinner every once in a while to a nice quite place to remind it how special it is), and its effect upon us as well as ours upon it. To arrive at this end, since we are still at the beginning, we will first examine the question of representation, followed by how we encounter these representations, and finally how they are related to their culture of origin as well as their culture of reception.

Keeping It Real

I personally blame Plato (the philosopher not the stuff you play with as a kid) for our current predicament. Were it not for this toga-wearing, wine-drinking, philosophizing, Athenian, we might not have to face the current division between reality and representation. You may be thinking to yourself, "Hey! I did not even realize that I face a division between reality and representation, and even if I do I don't much care about this Plato guy anyway." An astute observation to be sure, and one we will return to shortly, but first we will take Western philosophy seriously for a few minutes (after 2,500 years I suppose it could be worth a page or two).

Plato, in his famous work *The Republic* comes up with what is commonly referred to as the parable or allegory of the cave.[1] As the story goes, there are group of people chained inside a cave since birth, and positioned in such a way so that they can only look at the wall in front of them (note that there is no mention of how they got here, why they are here, what they eat, how they go to the bathroom, why no one has come looking for them, or any other question that would arise in the mind of anyone who was not a philosopher). Located behind the unfortunate folk chained in place is a fire, and between the fire and the oppressed people are a line of puppets that slowly move by casting shadows on the wall in front the philosophical prisoners. I know this sounds a bit more like a second-rate horror movie than philosophy, but stick with me here for another minute. The prisoners in this cave of despair watch the shadows go by and name them (they really do not have much else to do), and since this is the only thing they have ever known this is their reality. One day, let's say because the cave guard had a late night out in Athens and had one too many ouzo and fell asleep on the job, one of the prisoners is able to escape, and eventually makes his way out of the cave. Emerging from the cave (looking somewhat like an albino and with bones more fragile than glass due to the lack of sunlight), the prisoner would encounter the sun, see the shadows cast, the objects casting the shadows and would recognize that what he had known as real for his whole life was nothing but a representation.

Plato's point in writing this parable is to suggest that we need to move beyond the visual realm, beyond the realm of the tangible world, beyond the stuff of perception to the level of knowledge and understanding. The only way to do this is to recognize that the world that we see is limited and that it is a mere shadow and reflection of something higher, a realm of truth, and a world of ideas. We need to in the words of one of the great prophets of the twentieth century, Jim Morrison, to break on through to the other side. For Plato as well as many subsequent philosophers and the creators of *The Matrix* (one of the most philosophically unsound films of all times), the world that we inhabit is a representation of the real, not the real in itself. Implied in this view is that there is actually something real out there, separate from, beyond, above, outside, under, over, and through the woods, or which ever directional metaphor we choose to employ, which is different from our everyday experience. You may have thought that your book in your hands is actually a book, but according to the Platonic-influenced position assumed in much of Western philosophy, it is just a representation of a book. You can try this reasoning out next time you get pulled over ("No Officer, I wasn't speeding it was just the representation of speeding." But then you might just get charged with drunk driving).

We have determined that Plato was a strange fellow who, due to his fantasies of imprisoning people in caves, could have benefited from some therapeutic intervention, but this book is not about Greek philosophy or psychosis, so why does any of this matter? The problem of representation and reality that Plato documents in his parable of the cave remains alive and well in contemporary Western thought, and it lies in the background of many theories of media and television. The issue of what we are seeing when we watch TV, and that for the most part televised, or for that matter any mediated, images are viewed not as real, but as representations, echoes strongly of the parable of the cave (echoes, caves, get it?) This is to say that if we are going to discuss the interaction between television, identity, and communication, it would probably be good to know if what we are looking at is even real.

When cultural or media theorists emphasize the division between reality and representation they often do so with a fairly negative cast, accusing the representation of being nothing but an artifice,[2] a means of manipulation,[3] an attempt to assert power or control,[4] or some other variant that suggests that the world or reality in which we lived is open to being reformed or recast through different images or representations. The assumption here is that there are sinister forces at play, perhaps some type of cabal of old White men sitting about deciding who they want to oppress (or maybe it is Ronald McDonald, Mickey Mouse, and Rupert Murdoch, all sitting around a conference table drinking scotch and smoking cigars while trying to figure out how to control the world—the toys in the happy meals are actually homing devices). The point here is that the entire issue of ideology, control, manipulation, artifice, and subversion is based upon the assumption that what we watch is not real but rather a representation of the real that can be and often is manipulated.

The assumption that the televised image is less than real is curious for a couple of reasons. First, it is not quite clear what we encounter in the world that is not mediated. Except when we are infants, and have yet to acquire the language skills necessary for abstract thought and expres-. sion, there is no point in which we encounter an unmediated world (personally I might be willing to trade abstract thought for continuous playtime and long naps). William James expresses the idea that all encounters are mediated nicely in his foundational work on psychology by noting " . . . that men have no eyes but for those aspects of things which they have already been taught to discern."[5] What we see, or at least how we see it, is what we have been afforded the ability to see by our culture, community, and upbringing. When I see a big yellow "M," I see McDonald's; when I see red, white, and blue, I see America; and when I see Charlton Heston I see handgun violence. We will come back to this idea that we see what we have the eyes to see shortly, since it will be a central aspect of this book, but now what we need to recognize is that there does not seem to be any access to an unmediated reality. This is not to suggest that nothing is real, albeit as a student of Eastern religions I have my own suspicions, but rather that there is no point when our encounter of this real world is not somehow constructed by our culture (remember that whole point about our identity being tied into our culture—ah! yes, it is all coming together). Yes, televised images are more obviously constructed than our everyday encounter with the world, but it is a matter of degree and not kind.

The second reason that the division between reality and representation is problematic is that as constructed as the televised image may be, we, for the most part, encounter it as real enough. This is to say that as I sit watching *Lost* I do not trouble over the fact that the island is not a real place. I watch the show; I think about the show; I go online and read about it, blog about it, create a podcast for it; I discuss it with my friends, go to viewing parties for it, and sleep on sheets with depiction of the characters on them (this is all untrue, but I did have Scooby Doo sheets as a kid). In this sense, the televised image is as real to me, to the extent that I interact with it and it affects my life, as the coffee table on which my computer rests (which I suppose would make it a computer table). The idea that television is real enough and can affect the lives of those who encounter it has been the cause of considerable consternation among certain groups. Those in the Frankfurt school and other Marx-influenced thinkers saw our world as becoming commodified and feared that conformity would replace consciousness.[6] I always found this notion difficult to except, since unless the people writing about the all-consuming consciousness of TV were somehow smarter, better, stronger, faster, or just plain special, it is unclear how they could see beyond its all-consumingness (yes, of course, that is not a word). This is to say that if there is no place to stand outside, the all-consuming world of media, then you can divide through by the media and be left with reality.

The issue of representation and reality, specifically with regard to manipulation and control, is particularly exigent when examining the relationship between television, identity, and communication in a global age, because as we saw in the first chapter one of the prominent assumptions about globalization is that it is a form of Westernization, cultural imperialism, or the Disneyfication of the world. In accord with one of the central methodological points of this book, if we begin with this assumption, than we are almost guaranteed that what we will find will reinforce this idea, thereby clouding our ability to fully engage the subject at hand. There is little doubt that American culture, ideas, norms, mores, styles of dress, musical preferences, quirks, habits, and neurosis, are encoded in the media we produce. In truth, it could not be otherwise. Of course, *American Idol* conveys the insatiable appetite for stardom that pervades American culture, just as 24 displays the culture of fear that has been spawned by the existence of al-Qaida, the axis of evil, and Catholic priests. In the end the question is not whether these are imbued with American culture—they are. Nor is the question whether they are real or just representations—they are experienced as real enough. The question becomes, how are they received.

3–2–1 Contact

How media messages are received, has been, is, and likely will be one of the central focuses of media studies and is given particular attention with regard to the study of television. This issue has been at the forefront of a broader debate over the potential pernicious effects of television on the youth of today (conservative evangelical communities must have had a few minutes of spare time after their rallies against abortion, gay rights, women's rights, immigrant rights, and teletubbies). The basic argument runs something like this: Little Bobby just brought an automatic assault rifle to school and fired off more shots than a Los Angeles police officer during a traffic stop. Before the shooting spree, Bobby watched violent TV programs and played violent video games. Therefore, Bobby was influenced to treat his fellow students like ducks at a shooting range because of his viewing of violent programs and his playing of violent games. This form of argument, which suffers from both formal and informal logical fallacies (anyone take logic?), is both popular and persuasive in broader culture in large part because it is a simple and direct explanation of events. The argument does not take into account how Bobby was raised, why his parents let him view so much violent programming, possible developmental or psychological problems, the fact that he lives in a culture in which he had easy access to an assault rifle, or that he had likely demonstrated various other unusual behaviors (i.e., torturing small animals, pulling the heads off of dolls, listening to Brittney Spears) prior to committing this terrible act. If we do not take into account all of these other possible factors, then according to the initial argument, our streets should look like a shoot out at the *Ok Coral* due to the pervasive presence of violence on television. While America does have it share of gun violence (actually we have more than our share, perhaps we should give some to Canada), the streets are not rife with shootouts between men in business suits, and women lunching at country clubs (but it certainly is an amusing image).

The problem with the idea of how media messages are received presented above is threefold. First, much to bane and discontent of any first-year social science professor, it mistakes correlation for causation. This is to say that just because two things happen to occur around the same time, it does not mean that one causes the other. For example, I am currently sitting in a coffee shop in a wealthy suburb, watching women wearing designer workout clothes, carrying Louis Vuitton purses, and talking on their cell phones while looking haggard and confused because their nannies have the day off. While observing this phenomenon, I suddenly develop the urge to give up all of my worldly possessions and join an ashram in India or perhaps a Buddhist monastery in China (not that it would take much convincing anyway). A causational argument would suggest that it is the observation of American excess that called forth my desire to renounce the world. The correlational perspective would view my observation and reaction as related but would allow for the fact that there are other influences and factors at play, such as my fascination with Eastern religions, my aversion to capitalism, and my longstanding desire to wear nothing but robes and sandals.

The second problem with a causal argument about the effects of television is that it treats human beings as passive receptors of information. While there is little doubt that media messages can influence behavior, having an effect on everything from fashion to our understanding of

romantic relationships (I personally blame *Sex in the City* for ruining
the chances for true love for a entire generation), what this position
does not account for is what we are doing right now, thinking about
how we receive information. We may usually lead our lives in a largely
unreflective manner, choosing to enjoy the entrancing debauchery of
Desperate Housewives, rather than analyzing the representational form
of gender relationships in a postindustrial, andocentric world influenced
by Judeo-Christian morality, but we could do otherwise. We as rational
(or at least occasionally rational) creatures have the capacity to reflect on
the world, ourselves, our place in the world, and the world's place in us.
To assume that human beings are passive receptors of information and
that we merely accept as true or are directly influenced by everything we
see is to seriously call into question the nature of humanity itself. I may
have my serious doubts about the future of the human community, but
we have not reached the dystopian visions of Orwell or Huxley just yet.

The final problem with causal argument with regard to media reception, and stay with me here since we are about to come full circle, is that
to assume that a message has a particular effect is to assume that all
people encounter the image in the same way. The French literary critic
and philosopher Roland Barthes expresses this point well by pointing
out that all images are polysemous.[7] This neologism basically means that
there are various meanings, interpretations, and ways of encountering
any media image. For Barthes this idea remains fairly abstract (to be fair,
he is French) and is intended to remain a linguistic concept. I would like
to suggest (and I strongly urge you to agree, or I will make you actually
read his work) that the notion that media images are multivocal, or that
it speaks in multiple voices to different people or audiences often at the
same time, fits nicely with the concepts of culture and identity put forward in the previous chapter. Media, no matter what its form, is not
simply received, and is certainly not received in a universal way. Rather,
we as dynamic, reflexive people, who are inexorably tied to a cultural
world of meaning that is itself dynamic and fluid, are continually interacting with, reflecting on, shaping, appropriating, reforming, interpreting,
re-creating, manipulating, and even occasionally enjoying the media we
encounter. In other words, even if I were to have you all over to watch
TV and have some popcorn (I would need to get a far bigger apartment,
but I do have a popcorn popper), and we were to all sit and watch *Scrubs*

together, we would be watching the same show but seeing very different things. The fact that we all encounter things in a different way is not all that shocking. Clearly, the person who I passed on the street today who decided to bring back the 80s all by herself, leg warmers and all, and I have a vastly different encounter with fashion. The point that needs further consideration, particularly when we are discussing what happens when television crosses national borders, is how the variance in the reception in media texts and images is directly related to the inter-play of identity and culture. The difference between how I encounter a particular television show as a highly educated, charming, well-dressed, dashing young man (who clearly has a strong ego) and someone else of a similar educational, socioeconomic, and cultural background may not be that vast. If, however, I were to compare my encounter of the OC with that of someone who was reared in a fundamentalist Christian house-hold in rural Mississippi, the cultural worlds through which the program is interpreted and made sense of would create two fairly distinct pictures (mine being a pretty good time, and theirs being the fast path to the fires of hell). If this degree of cultural-identity variance can occur within our own great nation, how much more so must it be between the great defenders of truth and justice, and the godless communists of China or those folks who believe in all them gods in India.

Not So Secret Code

The British cultural theorist Stuart Hall provides an interesting way to help us understand how we as viewers can simultaneously receive and re-create media texts and images. Hall suggests that there are two sides to media communication, and I suppose by extension to any form of communication, encoding and decoding.[8] All forms of media from the educational articles in *Cosmo* that help us learn how to not make a fash-ion faux pas, to the educational programming on public television on which most of the hosts have clearly never read *Cosmo* are filtered through or encoded with a particular cultural frame, meaning, purpose, and intent. Once encoded, media forms are then transmitted and decoded by people who may or may not share the same cultural frame, and may or may not receive the intended meaning, purpose, or intent of the original encoded message. If, for example, I were to watch a commercial on TV for the new ½ pound, angus, flame-grilled burger at McDonald's, the likely purpose and intent of the commercial is to have me purchase and eat the said burger. However, as a longtime vegetarian, the way I decode that commercial is more akin to them asking me to slaughter helpless animals, destroy the rainforests, poison my body, and contribute to the starvation of millions around the world through the misuse of foodstuffs (I will now step off my soapbox and get back on topic). The point here is that it is unlikely those who created the McDonald's commercials would have wanted it to be received in the way I encountered it (unless of course they thought it would be funny to hire the people who do the marketing for PETA). In the end, what we have is a message sent and a message received that may not look very much alike except for the basic form.

Not all forms of decoding are alike, and according to Hall there are three basic types: dominant-hegemonic, negotiated, and oppositional.[9] Hall, being influenced by neo-Marxists or materialist thought that tends to view the world through such things as ideology, hegemony, superstructure, and class conflict, sees media messages as carrying a dominant ideological idea operating within a broader hegemonic discourse. This is not nearly as confusing as it sounds, but academics need to compensate for being picked last in gym class when they were kids through exercising their large craniums as adults. Basically, media is created with a particular motive, intent, and purpose, and we can either accept it completely (dominant-hegemonic), accept parts of it and rethink others (negotiated), or completely reject it or reform/recreate it (oppositional). Let's take an example. Let's say that former president Bush makes an address to the nation about the war on terror (something that I never actually understood, since I am unsure how you engage in active warfare against an emotion. Perhaps when a child is feeling afraid of the dark Special Force troops storm through his door guns blazing and start shooting the dark). In this case, the position of hegemonic decoding would be held by a lifelong Republican from Texas who accepts the former president at his word, exactly as it is said (as incoherent as it may be). The position of negotiated decoding would be held by an Independent voter in Missouri who accepts the basic premise of the former president's position, "fighting the evil doers over there so that we can keep shopping over here," but disagrees with certain points or details. The final possibility, that of oppositional decoding, would be held by a New York Democrat, who would disagree with the former president no matter what he said, even if it was something as obvious as we need air to live.

The three possible forms of decoding offered by Hall are interesting and fairly useful within a given cultural or ideological frame. What he does not account for, however, and what is central to this book, is what happens when media travels beyond the boundaries of its culture of origin. If I were to sit and watch Bollywood movies, even as someone who has traveled widely through India, has long studied Indian religions and cultures, would happily eat South Indian food for every meal, and has even been mistaken as Indian by Indians (which admittedly is a bit confusing considering I am of Eastern European Jewish descent), it would not be a question of acceptance, negotiation, or rejection. In truth, it would be a question of decontextualized confusion, misunderstanding, and reinterpretation. All of those gyrating bodies moving together in choreographed routines that make Broadway look like a talent show at a school for children without rhythm do not have me either accept or reject the complex gender dynamics embedded in Indian culture. As a foreign viewer what I decode is something exotic, occasionally tantalizing, and always thoroughly amusing (except after being sick in bed for three days with nothing else to watch, at which point it quickly moves from amusing to terrifying—perhaps we can wage a war on it). What is encoded within a given culture becomes something wholly other when it moves beyond its original boundaries.

Speaking in Many Voices

The reason why media is able to become wholly other when it crosses cultural boundaries is that there is not an inherent connection between either images or words and what they represent. The reason that an apple is called an apple and not *plubarb* is purely arbitrary (*plubarb* would be more fun to say). The fact that if we see a seductive woman biting into an apple we register biblical allusions is only due to our culture, not something inherent in the apple. And the expression "as American as apple pie" could be a metaphor for anything from America being warm and comforting to being excellent with a side of ice cream, for those who have never before encountered it. This is to say that the words and metaphors we use, the same ones that get embedded or encoded into our media are culturally specific, and that, once they leave our borders, how they are received and understood is open to more interpretation than a David Lynch movie (I watched *Lost Highway* seven times before I realized that it doesn't actually have anything to do with highways). The multivocal nature of media allows for a broad array of encounters, meanings, interpretations, and forms of reception as it moves between its culture of origin and its final audience.

The idea that media messages, when they cross cultural borders, are multivocal, and are open to various forms of reinterpretation and re-creation in light of the lack of universal meaning suggests that we should add another category to the three provided by Stuart Hall, that of misunderstanding. It is not that people in cultures other than that which produced the original media form cannot understand it as it was intended (it is not like me with Calculus, where once there are no longer numbers in math I treat it like an English class and just rearrange the words and variables to form Haikus). Rather, misunderstanding means that, at least initially, a distinct set of cultural metaphors will be placed upon the foreign media form, arriving at an encounter and interpretation that may have little to do with the original intent. Misunderstanding is not the same as incommensurability. We can move toward understanding the media in common, but it takes a significant amount of effort, something that just sounds tiring and makes me want to pull out the graham crackers and apple juice and take a nap. We will come back to the difficult work of moving from misunderstanding to understanding in the last chapter of the book (hopefully after a nice long rest—perhaps a nice trip to the Bahamas—you can keep reading on the Beach).

As the audience for a television program or any other media form we are receiving a message and simultaneously responding to it by either accepting it, accepting parts of it, rejecting it, or misunderstanding it. Sometimes these categories may overlap, and we will simultaneously reject and misunderstand part of a message. Think of a speech by Barak Obama. When he utters cryptically, "We are the ones we have been waiting for," I have less a sense of what he means than I do about string theory (unless of course he is enlightened and speaking to the condition of the unification of being and time, sort of like string theory—somehow doubtful). At the same time that I scratch my head in a stupor at my confusion over his message, I simultaneously reject what he is saying, even though I do not understand it—it just somehow seems wrong (I mean the last time a charismatic speaker drew a crowd of 200,000 in Berlin it did not really work out very well). This is all to say that these categories are not mutually exclusive and that even when media crosses cultural boundaries, while misunderstanding may be particularly common, there will be a variety of complex encounters that are not properly accounted for by any simple idea. If media tends to be misunderstood when it crosses cultural boundaries—and as we discussed in Chapter 1, cultures are dynamic, complex, and not monolithic—it seems as though it would be more difficult to study the interaction between television and other cultures than it would be to go to Disney World without buying Mickey Mouse ears (I have a pair in my office with Dr. Sherman on them).

Drink the Kool-Aid

Having outlined the relationship between culture and identity as well as the relationship between the audience and media, we are now in a position to offer a profound and radical method for the study of television across cultures: watch television. Well, at least that is step number one. As obvious as it sounds you cannot properly understand the relationship between television, culture, identity, and communication if you do not sit down and watch the programs. If you are not laughing with or at American Idol and calling in 7,345 times a night to vote for your favorite contestant, you are just not getting the full glory of the experience. If you are not sitting on the edge of your seat, heart pounding, ready to jump off your couch and help Jack Bauer, then you are not truly embracing the jingoistic paranoia of 24. And if you do not snicker at America while watching the cultural decay embodied in the Simpsons, then you are not fully encountering the wonders of Springfield. The first step to understanding television is to allow yourself to actually encounter it without judgment, disdain, concern, trepidation, horror, indignity, or any other form of judgment. Go ahead, drink the Kool-Aid and enjoy the trip.

We need to drink the Kool-Aid, because that is what the majority of people who watch television in the great nation of America as well as around the rest of the world are doing. I do not imagine that if we were to walk into an average home in Thiruvananthapuram, India (go ahead, just try and pronounce it), we would find a family sitting around discussing the capitalist tendencies of Rupert Murdoch and the effect that it has on Star broadcasting in India. It would be far more likely that we would find them watching the TV and actually enjoying the programs, once they overcame the shock of having random strangers walk into their home.

If we want to understand the dynamic relationship between television, culture, and identity we should begin by recognizing that television audiences are just like you and I (as frightening as that may be) and not some mass of people being controlled, manipulated, cajoled, persuaded, convinced, brainwashed, or otherwise lured into a hypnotic state by some evil cabal of old White men trying to dominate the world. Sorry to be the one who has to break it to you, but all of the evils of the world from global warming to Roller disco cannot be blamed on "them" or "they" because we are "them" and "they." We are the ones creating advertisements, crafting programs, writing magazine articles, running corporations, holding political office, and occupying every other role that "they," "them," or the "people" in power supposedly do. The problem is that even in the great bastion of capitalism, democracy, and Ronald McDonald, certain elements of Marxist thought seem to die hard (I think someone needs to go tell the professors at the Ivy League universities that the Soviet Union collapsed and that it did not really work out very well). Neo-Marxist materialist thought has had a strong influence on the study of culture and media and because of this we tend to assume that there will be the powerful and the powerless, those in control and those under control, the elite and the masses, the strong and the weak, and that those who are powerless, weak, under control are the masses who watch television and through this are controlled by the elite. Unfortunately, this assumption about the human condition is more misleading than a map without names.

Getting to Know You, Getting to Know All about You

There have been two primary camps in the field of cultural studies, one that tends to focus on the structure of cultures and another that tends to focus on the content of cultures. It is as if we were comparing two companies—in this instance, let's say Wal-Mart and Whole Foods. From a structuralist perspective, we would examine the trappings of the companies: both have CEOs, presidents, vice-presidents, marketing departments, secretaries, buyers, stores, sales people, stock rooms, and places to eat. So, from a purely structural perspective, they sound fairly similar. If, however, we assume a culturalist perspective and look at the content, things begin to appear a bit differently. The marketing department at one is targeting Birkenstock-wearing, highly educated, hybrid-driving, Dave Matthews Band–listening, granola-eating liberals. While the other is aiming for flag-waving, pick-up-truck-driving, god-fearing, Lynard Skinard–listening, Jimmy Dean sausage–eating, Middle Americans. The stores of the one are filled with strange-sounding products like quinoa, tofurky, and organic cherimoya, decorated in natural tones, and filled with employees who look like they just came out of the Woodstock movie. The other companies stores are filled with giant bags of potato chips, Twinkies, and Wonder Bread, decorated in . . . well, not decorated, and staffed by employees in blue vests who look like they are one step away from committing a shopping cart–related homicide. If we were to simply look at the structure of these companies we would miss some of the most critical and telling information. It is only by considering them in their specificity and particularity that we truly begin to get a sense of what they are.

To properly understand the interaction between American media and other cultures, particularly cultures so wholly different than our own, like China and India, we need to look beyond the structural elements and engage in an act of cultural tracking. To the extent that culture and identity are directly and inexorably intertwined, to understand the one is to understand the other. It is like fire and heat, water and wetness, and Bert and Ernie (who I always found a little creepy); you just cannot have one without the other. This said, the study of television across cultural boundaries demands, and here is the obvious point, that we know something about the foreign cultures. As Raymond Williams once noted, we should not assume that there is a direct relationship between the media product and the mindset of the consumer.[10] Because of this, it is not enough to try to look for the influence of American media, since, as we have noted before, we tend to find exactly what we are looking for. Rather, recognizing that culture and identity are dynamic and that media is multivocal, particularly when it crosses cultural boundaries, we need to look to the culture of reception to begin to understand what cultural metaphors and interpretations they may be placing upon it. We Americans are great and all, but it may not hurt to know something about other cultures.

The problem with trying to understand another culture is that, as was noted in the last chapter, they tend to be dynamic, complex, and not internally consistent. One of my great joys of being a teacher is my ability to torment my students by asking them questions that they cannot possibly answer. During a conversation about modern nationalism I asked them to try to define what it means to be American. Their first answers included such things as freedom, democracy, and equal rights, at which point I subtly reminded them that these things are sort of shared by the majority of developed nations (and that the equal-rights part is somewhat ironic at best in a country that has secret military prisons, a significant number of citizens without medical care, and a educational system that fails a vast number of our citizens). After calling me a *liberal hippie*, the students answers changed, and focused more on things like choice, difference, and diversity. At which point, after having stopped eating my granola and put down my copy of *The Nation*, I asked them how it was that we could define the American identity in terms of diversity and difference. The conversation ended with the students being befuddled by how we can be united by what divides us, and me feeling as though I should stop wearing tie dye to class.

Due to its geographical, economic, ethnic, and religious diversity, America does present a particularly difficult case when it comes to offering a clear sense of its culture or identity. It is not immediately obvious what unites me as an overeducated hippie living in New York City, with a Southern belle from Mississippi, and a homosexual African American from Chicago (they are actually all related in a very strange six degrees of Kevin Bacon sort of way—maybe you will be able to figure it out by the end of the book). The problem is not, however, just synchronic (difference occurring at the same time), it is also diachronic (differences occurring across time). American culture is not what it was or what it will be, it is what it is. This what-it-is-ness of American culture will become that what-it-was-ness as soon as it is experienced, and the what-it-will-be-ness, while never able to be predicted, will become the what-it-is-ness that will then become the what-it-was-ness and ad infinitum. This is to say that the diversity within a given culture along with its dynamic nature across time (this is, of course, if you accept linear time, which I do not, since I find it rather oppressive) make it such that it is unclear how we can say anything at all about any culture. And yet, as diverse as American culture may be, if you were to put me in front of a line-up I could still somehow pick out the American.

Even though cultures are not internally consistent and are open to significant change and reformation over time, it is still possible to have what the literary critic and philosopher Isaiah Berlin once call a "sense of reality."[11] What Berlin means by this is that we each are an embodiment of a vast cultural body that we do not even recognize or know that we know. It is everything from how we greet each other, the distance we stand from one another, and the length of time that you look into someone else's eyes, to our shared symbols, practices, and rituals. Most of this stuff that allows us to have a sense of our world or culture remains largely below the level of everyday awareness, but that does not make it any less present or real (like Santa Claus or the Easter bunny). In a similar vein if I were to put a McDonald's, Wendy's, and Burger King hamburger in front of you (better you than me), the packaging would look different, and the burgers themselves would look, smell, and taste different, and yet despite the differences, once you overcame the intense feeling of nausea from having to eat all of that heart attack–inducing food, you would certainly say that they are all hamburgers. Similarly aspects of a given culture may appear differently, and yet there remains a sense in which we can recognize them as part of the same larger phenomenon.

In the chapter to follow we will begin to workout a sense of Chinese culture and the status of its media industry so as to begin to gain a better understanding of what happens when American television leaves the amber waves of grain and purple mountains majesty of our beautiful land and arrives in the land of Mongol invaders, Mao, and the factory that built my iPod. To study television and identity in today's world is to move beyond old structuralist or neo-Marxist materialists models and to jump into the wonderfully confusing, chaotic, and disorienting space of other cultures, peoples, and ways of being. Since I cannot afford to bring you all with me and I would not want you to have to get all the vaccinations or take the strange malaria medication that induces hallucinations (occasionally fun yes, but not what you need when you are in the middle of a sea of people and it is 137 degrees in the shade), I will take the journey myself and report back. Hopefully we can get a sense of modern China—that is if I don't get arrested.

Stay tuned things could get exciting.

Notes

1. Plato. *The Republic*. Penguin Classics, 2007.
2. Caldwell, John Thornton. *Televisuality: Style, Crisis, and Authority in American Television*. Rutgers University Press, 1995.
3. Lull, James. *Media, Communication, Culture*. Polity Press, 1995.
4. Foucault, Michel. *Discipline & Punish: The Birth of the Prison*. Vintage, 1995.
5. James, William. *The Principles of Psychology, Vol. 1*. 1st ed. Cosimo Classics, 2007, p. 443.
6. Creeber, Glen. *Tele-visions: An Introduction to Television Studies*. British Film Institute, 2006, p. 46.
7. Evans, Jessica, and Stuart Hall. *Visual Culture: The Reader*. 1st ed. Sage Publications Ltd, 1999.
8. Hall, Stuart. *Culture, Media, Language*. HarperCollins Publishers Ltd, 1980.
9. Ibid, pp. 136–8.
10. Higgins, John. *The Raymond Williams Reader*. Wiley-Blackwell, 2001.
11. Berlin, Isaiah. *The Sense of Reality: Studies in Ideas and Their History*. Farrar, Straus and Giroux, 1998.

Suggestions for Further Reading

Berlin, Isaiah. *The Sense of Reality: Studies in Ideas and Their History*. Farrar, Straus and Giroux, 1998.
Caldwell, John Thornton. *Televisuality: Style, Crisis, and Authority in American Television*. Rutgers University Press, 1995.
Creeber, Glen. *Tele-visions: An Introduction to Television Studies*. British Film Institute, 2006.

Evans, Jessica, and Stuart Hall. *Visual Culture: The Reader.* 1st ed. Sage Publications Ltd, 1999.

Foucault, Michel. *Discipline & Punish: The Birth of the Prison.* Vintage, 1995.

Hall, Stuart. *Culture, Media, Language.* HarperCollins Publishers Ltd, 1980.

Havens, Timothy. *Global Television Marketplace.* British Film Institute, 2006.

James, William. *The Principles of Psychology,* Vol. 1. 1st ed. Cosimo Classics, 2007.

Lull, James. *Media, Communication, Culture.* Polity Press, 1995.

Parks, Lisa, and Shanti Kumar. *Planet TV: A Global Television Reader.* NYU Press, 2002.1.

3

A Slow Boat to China

Exercise #3

Take a deep breath in, feel the air fill your body, and then breath out releasing all tension, anxiety, worry, fear, longing, desire, concern, anger, and attachment. Now that you have realized the deepest truths of the Buddha (at least momentarily—but then, I suppose that in itself is part of the Buddhist message), and your mind is clearer than the waters of a mountain spring, you are ready for the next exercise. Take out a piece of paper, and write down anything and everything that comes to mind when your hear the word China (don't worry, no one else is going to read what you wrote so you can be as honest, direct, and politically incorrect as you want).

(You can try http://www.asianclassicalmp3.org/amoy.htm for a nice background soundtrack.)

Look over your list and try to organize your answers into groupings or categories. Did you take note of the physical characteristics of the people or the manner of dress (come on, we all remember the games we played as children)? Did pictures of the architecture or physical landscape fill your mind with dreams of travel to foreign lands? Or perhaps your mind moved more toward the ethereal aspects of Chinese religion and culture, and had you write down the prophetic verses of the great philosopher of fortune cookies, Confucius. There may have been some who, motivated by hunger, thought of nothing but *mu shoo* and scallion pancakes (I really must have a thing for pancake-shaped food). And other people who are nostalgic for the good old days of the Communist revolutions may have thought about the Chinese political situation. Since we are already playing with categories (which is not as much fun as Hungry-Hungry Hippos but will have to do for now) take a few minutes and try to write something down for each of the following things: history, culture, religion, politics, geography, economics, demographics, and cuisine (I have to get something in about food).

(If you are tired of the classical Chinese music you can try looking up the Bjork of China, Sa Ding Ding) Not that you are being graded on this, since as we all know the value of the work is in the effort and not the outcome (even thinking about that brings back terrible memories of childhood sports—"Go ahead do the best you can." "Okay, but the best I can do is strike out or get hit with the ball."), but look at your list and think about how you did. Was this exercise difficult for you? Did you arrive mostly at stereotypes and caricatures? Considering China is often touted as the world's growing superpower (though I can't figure out which super power it has, maybe the ability to grow infinitely large), and is frequently in the news in terms of trade issues and human rights abuses, is it surprising that we know so little about it? If you were able to fill in these categories, where did you come by your information, and what was the intention of the person writing or broadcasting it (I, of course, am motivated by nothing but the highest virtue and love of knowledge).

Ni hao

Welcome to China. I am feeling a bit jet lagged, hungry (the airplane food was, well, airplane food), disoriented, could use a shower, and have a nauseous feeling that hovers somewhere between having been on a merry-go-round for 27 hours and being on a rickety, old row boat in a tropical storm. All that aside, the trip has gone fairly well, and I have arrived safely into the ultramodern, eerily quiet, hyper-clean, shiny, new Shanghai international airport. After passing through immigration and feeling somewhat slighted that they did not pull me aside for questioning since I feel as though I look like a suspicious character, collecting my luggage, and buying a bottle of water that goes by the curious and yet oddly amusing brand name Limpid (I always prefer my water strong and vibrant), I prepare myself to step outside to get a breath of fresh air. Well, it is a breath of something, but calling it fresh would be like calling Paris Hilton an actress. The temperature outside is near 105 degrees, the air is so thick that it feels like walking through a steam bath, and there is so much pollution and haze that the sun looks a flashlight being shone through Vaseline.

Realizing that I really should travel to countries that will not cause me to sweat through my clothing (Iceland seems nice), I decide to track down the express train that runs from the airport to downtown Shanghai. After developing a case of asthma, asking 14 people how to get there, and trying to decipher the meaning of the English on the signs, I finally board the train that looks oddly like the monorail at Disney World. Unlike the monorail at Disney World, however, this train moves so fast that it makes the cars on the road next to it look as though they are going backwards. Reaching 430 kilometers per hour (that translates to really fast in miles per hour), the train hurtles through the outlying areas of city, past a landscape of apartment complexes, shopping malls, and not one panda bear or dragon. While it is certainly fascinating to break the land-speed record during my travels, it is probably not what I need in my current state of nausea and disorientation. What feels like 53 hours after leaving my apartment, I finally find my hotel, and rather than being greeted by traditional architecture, people in cute little Communist outfits, or oppressed followers of Falun Gong, I come to find that I am staying above a Starbucks. I am beginning to think that China may not be exactly what I expected.

China is a curious place. This is, of course, from the perspective of someone reared in the greatest of all countries in the world, an ardent lover of capitalism, and firm believer in truth (except when it is inconvenient), justice (except for them terrorists), equality (except for women and minorities), and the American way (except for immigrants). From the American perspective, any country that has a one-party Communist government, that has been accused of numerous human rights abuses, that has engaged in the active suppression of religion and minority groups, and where the average yearly salary is less than the average weekly salary of most Western countries will certainly be viewed as a bit off the mark. The interesting thing, however, is that one of the most curious things about China is that it defies the majority of Western stereotypes and expectations. Rather than being filled with dutiful Communist workers or kung-fu fighting, China is a rapidly modernizing economic power whose cities are filled with shiny new skyscrapers, fashion-conscious youth, and a growing John Waynesque self-certain swagger.

Before we can understand modern China and its relation to and understanding of American television, it would first be useful to have a sense of the religious, cultural, and historical forces that have allowed for its development and continue to exert influence. As was noted in the previous chapters (if you can remember that far back), while cultures are not internally consistent and are open to continual change and reformation, there are still many family resemblances that interact with identity. This is to say that everything that follows may not apply to all people all of the time, or all people some of the time, or all people in all times, or to people who are people only sometime, and especially not to all people not in time, but it can still serve as a general framework that affords some degree of insight and understanding into the overdetermined, complex, multifaceted, and continually developing and variable phenomenon of Chinese culture.

Confucius Says

Confucius says, "A good place to start is with Confucius." While folk religion and pantheistic and polytheistic beliefs and practices have existed in China, as elsewhere, since the origins of civilization itself, Confucius and the subsequent religion—or some would say philosophy—of Confucianism is the first organized body of religious thought to become a significant lasting influence on Chinese culture. Somewhere around 551 BCE a fellow was born who would come to be known as Confucius, which is an English transliteration of Kong Fuzi (Master Kong) that is in turn a transliteration of the original Chinese, which I will not write, because it makes my computer think that I am speaking in tongues (an occasional occurrence to be sure, but only while handling snakes in the Appalachian Mountains). Confucius, much like many other prophetic figures (Jesus, Joseph Smith, Jim Morrison, etc.), was not fully appreciated or widely accepted in his own day. While he did attract a small following of students who did record many of his teaching and maxims, much to the gratitude of future fortune-cookie makers, his influence grew slowly over the generations to come. Confucianism remains one of the big three religions in China (I like the idea of organizing religions into something akin to the NCAA basketball conference. "And here Jesus has the ball, and he hands it off to the Buddha because he believes in giving to the meek and poor. But Buddha refuses the ball because he says it doesn't exist.") and still to this day you can go to Qufu (pronounced something like Choo Foo) and see the birthplace of Confucius (which today seems a bit more like an amusement park than a religious site).

Confucianism is fairly distinct from the Western religious traditions in the sense that it concerns itself neither with arguments about god or excessive amounts of ritual. It is not dogmatic, does not posses an institutional hierarchy (No popes, cardinals, bishops, deacons, grand mufti, chief rabbis, or apostles—yup, the Mormons still have 12 of them), and does not demand the profession on specific creeds or articles of faith. Confucianism focuses on issues of familial and social relationships, governance, education, and ethics, which is why some consider it to be more of a system of philosophy than a religion (a point that we can save for a cantankerous, and yet somehow simultaneously coma-inducing, academic debate). In a sense, the fundamental concern of Confucianism is learning how to be human (it is far less obvious than it appears) and encourages followers to realize this path through a greater awareness of our networks of relationships and how we come to be through these relationships. Rather than thinking of themselves as self-created, isolated, individuals, as we tend to in the good ol' US of A, those influenced by the Confucian tradition would describe themselves more in terms of their social relationships. Whereas I might answer the question "who are you?" with my name, or when in New York, perhaps with "Who the hell do you think you are?," the Confucian answer would likely be closer to a list of significant relationships such as the son of John and Jane, the brother of Mary, the husband of Buffy, and an employee of Stark Industries.

Confucius emphasized not only the centrality of relationships but also the need to maintain harmony within our personal, social, and political relationships. When asked to supply a guiding principle of conduct, Confucius once replied, "To look at nothing in defiance of ritual, to hear nothing in defiance of ritual, to speak of nothing in defiance of ritual [and] to undertake nothing in defiance of ritual."[1] While this could sound to Western ears akin to saying "obey!" the connotation in China is slightly more subtle. It is a bit difficult for those of us raised under the influence MTV, reality television, self-help books, and life coaches to recognize the difference between social harmony and social imposition, but for those slightly less addicted to the heroin of Western society known as individualism, the idea of putting the social before the personal is not all that strange. To put this another way, for those raised under a Confucian influence, the very things that we hold most dear, personal freedom and choice, may not even be meaningful ideas.

Another significant aspect of the Confucian tradition that is conspicuously absent from the American landscape is humility. The American myth is one of achievement and the ability of all people to be the best if they put in the time and effort. How this would work is not exactly clear since if everyone were President or the CEO of a major company (an odd standard of achievement since both positions rank fairly low in social esteem due to their tendency toward Machiavellian machinations), it is unclear who would take out the garbage, deliver the mail, work in restaurants, teach the future generations, or manage any other daily task that keeps society functioning. Recognizing the relational nature of human being, the goal of harmony, and perhaps the fact that he likes having someone to make him his morning latte Confucius suggests that "The great man is dignified but never haughty [while the] petty man is haughty but never dignified."[2] This perspective does not do away with hierarchy, but rather recognizes the value and importance of equal respect and dignity (imagine that).

Act without Acting

Much as Confucius was a man of order, harmony, and humility, his possible contemporary (possible because it is debated whether he actually existed at all or was merely a composite of various figures— sort of like Bush who, while physically exists, is basically just a mental composite of Cheney, Rumsfeld, Leo Strauss, and Ayn Rand) Lao Tzu was also concerned with harmony and order, but arrived at it from a different direction. For our imaginary friend Lao Tzu, order and harmony were to be found in nature in something called the way or the Tao " . . . which is the source of all being and governor of all life, human and natural, and the basic undivided unity in which all the contradictions and distinctions of existence are ultimately resolved."[3] The Tao can perhaps be best understood as path and not a thing. The Tao is not god; it is not an incarnation of god, it is not a doctrine, creed, first principle, or type of chicken at a Chinese restaurant (which by the way does not exist in restaurants in China, making me think that this General Tao maybe me a reincarnation of Colonel Sanders). Defining Tao or Taoism is rather tricky because as the very first passage of the Tao-te Ching (the most significant of Taoist writings) states, "The Tao that can be told of is not the eternal Tao."[4] That said we are left in the awkward position of trying to speak about the unspeakable, a job more challenging than getting the President of Iran to have a sleepover party with the Prime Minister of Israel (perhaps all global conflict should be resolved through pillow fights).

For all the things that cannot be said about Taoism we can still look at a couple of its significant elements and see how they might influence Chinese thought and culture. The first point, and this may seem a tad ironic in light of China's current asthma-inducing levels of pollution, is that there is a strong appreciation of nature. Whereas Confucianism seeks harmony in and through our social relationship, Taoism tends to step back and say something to the effect of, "Uh, yeah, that whole human social interaction thing isn't really working out so well, so maybe we should look for harmony in nature instead." Had Thoreau been living in China he definitely would have stood firmly in the Taoist camp (and he was, in fact, a fan of Eastern religions—he was known for wearing t-shirts that say, "I love Vishnu"). For Taoism, harmony is to be found in nature, and in our aligning ourselves with the way of Tao that is embodied in the world. In another passage in the Tao-te Ching, humanity is encouraged to "Manifest plainness, embrace simplicity, reduce selfishness, [and] have few desires."[5] These words, which would make any good red-blooded American recoil faster than a long-tail cat from a rocking chair, imply that the goals of life are best attained not through material ends, but rather through the rejection of those ends.

Another interesting aspect of Taoism is its tendency to play upon what appears to us Western folk as contradictions or paradoxes. A nice example of this is found in the writings of the fourth-century BCE Taoist thinker Chuang Tzu when he states, "Heaven produces nothing, yet all life is transformed; Earth does not support, yet all life is sustained; the emperor and the king take actionless action, yet the whole world is served."[6] The initial reaction to these lines by those reared in the world of linear time and scientific rationality might be something like, "that damn hippie needs to stay off the drugs," but within a different frame these same lines may actually be deeply meaningful. In a fascinating work, Richard Nisbett suggests that one of the primary differences between Western and Eastern thinking is that while we tend to see one thing at a time in a fairly linear way and quickly place things into either/ or type categories (black or white, right or wrong, extra crispy or original recipe) East Asians have a proclivity for holding multiple stimuli simultaneously and not putting them into oppositional categories (original recipe and extra crispy in the same bucket).[7] This is to say that patterns of thought influenced by the Taoist tradition are more likely to view the world as determined by multiple, coexisting factors that we may view as unable to coexist.

Rub My Belly

One final figure needs to be introduced in order to complete the tripartite religious/cultural background influences of China: the Buddha. Unlike our friend Confucius and our imaginary friend Lao Tzu, the Buddha was not a native of China, but did live around the same time as the other two (which is itself interesting, since this era of human history seemed to has more philosophical and religious reformers than the 90s had boy bands). Buddhism did not become influential in china until sometime around the fifth or sixth century CE and slowly became a significant influence throughout the country. As the teachings of the pot-bellied prince spread through China they, like all religious thought that moves beyond its boundaries, shifted, adapted, and were re-imagined to fit with the Chinese traditions. While we do not have the time to pick apart the complex inner workings of Buddhist theology and practices as they splintered into distinct traditions (I grow sleepy even thinking about writing it), we can still look at few basic ideas that can help us complete our paint by numbers picture of China. The Buddha, who by today's clinical standards may have been diagnosed as clinically depressed due his rather pessimistic outlook on human affairs, offered four noble truths: (1) Life is suffering, (2) suffering is caused by desire and attachment, (3) desire and attachment can be destroyed, and (4) they can be destroyed through the eightfold path. While not the cheeriest estimation of human existence, it does offer hope for liberation if we follow the following eight steps (as opposed to freedom from alcohol through 12 steps): right understanding, right purpose, right speech, right conduct, right vocation, right effort, right alertness, and right concentration. Those of us reared in the land of instant gratification, drive-through liquor stores, and online grocery shopping may not take well to a system that demands quite that much effort—we tend to prefer our salvation to come in more manageable pieces, like 1 hour at church on Sunday, followed by pancakes at Cracker Barrel. Beyond the effort aspect, the other part that may seem a bit curious to us is the fact that the source of all suffering is desire and attachment. We in the West tend to take a slightly different approach and try to buy our way to heaven through acquiring as much stuff as possible (an odd quirk of protestant theology that was picked up by those oh so cute, but not actually very friendly, pilgrims that founded this country). As strange as it may seem, nonattachment and simplicity in livelihood and action are actually held in high esteem in the Buddhist tradition.

Another important aspect of Buddhism as it has been practiced in China is compassion, something stemming from the Mahayana tradition (okay, just a bit of abstract Buddhist theology). According to Mahayana tradition, beside just the Buddha are also people who are Buddha like but who do something that is nearly unthinkable in the Western traditions, put aside their own salvation for the sake of other. These anathemas to Western consciousness are known as Bodhisattvas—one of the most popular in China being Guanyin, the Bodhisattva of compassion. According to the Bodhisattva vow, "It is through his compassionate skill in means that he is tied to the world, and that though he has attained the state of a saint, yet he appears to be in the state of an ordinary person."[8] Something particularly striking about this idea is that it conveys a sense that it is not every man for himself, or even one for another, but rather all for all. It is as though we are on a sinking ship and one person sees a life raft. If he takes it himself he will survive, but would not be able to safely get across the sea. If, however, that man saves the other people on the boat, there will be enough people in the life raft to help get safely to the other side of the ocean (an unlikely scenario in America since, due to the obesity epidemic, we might not all fit on the boat—I always new that McDonald's was in league with the devil).

What we see arising from even this limited look at Buddhism is a picture in which material stuff might actually be more of a burden than a boon and accordingly cooperation trumps competition (an idea that would cause the cigars to drop out of the mouths of the Ayn Rand–influenced neoconservatives). While the Buddha might be an apostate to the American dream, his ideas fit nicely with those of Confucius and Lao Tzu. For these men, the social is primary over the individual; harmony should always be sought over competition, and the world cannot be divided into simple either/or categories. In a sense what we arrive at is not simply a different way of looking at the world (I think that crayon in more sky blue than periwinkle), but entirely different patterns of thought and ways of engaging the world (I think the crayon should be grouped with other blue things rather than other crayons). Or as Richard Nisbett puts it, the Western and Eastern worldviews "... include profoundly different social relations, views about the nature of the world, and characteristic thought processes."[9] This is a King Kong–sized claim, which draws upon so many psychological and philosophical assumptions that it would take another 17 books just to try to explain (which if you are interested in reading you can contact my publisher with letters of praise and requests for future books on my behalf), but it is one worth keeping in mind as we try to understand the Chinese encounter with American television and how they come to understand America and the American identity.

The Little Red (Section of This) Book

We are now going to take a bit of a step forward in history by about 1,400 years. As much as the history teacher in me is aghast at taking such a step, my OCD side is forcing me to keep things neat, tidy, and to the point, and to the point, and to the point. . . . In no way do I mean to dismiss the importance of Chinese history, or make this a history of great, or imaginary men, but rather I am trying to give a sense of the influences on contemporary Chinese culture without having to write another book (the other 17 are still on hold). By taking this great leap forward (extra points if you get the reference) we will arrive just shy of modern-day China, into an era marked by revolution, war, and political turmoil. Out of this Chinese revolution that raged between 1926 and 1950 arose one man who would shape the development of China for the next half century, the man so well known that he can pull a Madonna and go by only one name, Mao.

Mao and the associated form of political thought that came to bear his name Maoism were the primary influences in China from 1950 until his death in 1976. Mao was strongly influenced by Marxist-Leninist thought (but then who hasn't been), but saw the need to adapt the Communist model to fit the current economic and political realities of China. One of the major early differences between Mao and his contemporaries over in Red Square is that the slogan of the party should not be "Workers of the world unite," but rather "Peasants of the world unite!" China was not an industrialized country during the early twentieth century and, therefore, did not have the industrial worker base to lead a revolution as originally conceived by Marx or Lenin—or at least it would have been a very small and short-lived revolution (9:23 a.m. March 25, 1926, the revolution begins—9:27 a.m., the revolutionary force of Bob, Frank, and Henry has been crushed). Since there was no industrial base, Mao turned to what China did have and till this day still has in great number, rural peasants. This is to say that Maoist thought in China was always attached to an agrarian and rural ideal, something that can readily be seen in the charming propaganda posters of the era, which have today become little more than kitsch sold primarily to Western tourists (personally I prefer the Mao alarm clocks where he waves at you as the seconds tick by). This adulation of the peasant life shaped China economically and politically for a generation and would place the land of Pandas and pagodas in a difficult position when Mao died in 1976.

After the political revolution was won, Mao felt it necessary to engage in another form of revolution, perhaps because he enjoyed ferris wheels and merry-go-rounds so much as a child (get it, revolving things).

The cultural revolution that took place between 1966 and 1969 or 1976 depending on who you ask (again the stuff of overheated debates in very boring seminars) and was in its most basic form an attempt by Mao to purge China of old customs, ideas, habits, and culture. Putting aside the countless deaths, oppression, and loss of political freedom caused by the revolution, there really are few better ways to get to social harmony than by doing away with all forms of disagreement. Mao had two primary targets that he wished to do away with: everything old, and everything foreign (everything happening immediately in the present in China was fine, as long as it did not reference anything old, or foreign, or anyone who disagreed, or anyone who Mao didn't like). If carried to its logical end, this type of revolution would breed a culture that was continuously reinventing itself and inherently suspicious of outside influence. For those who have been to modern Chinese cities and seen skyscrapers towering over temples this may seem about right.

One final point about Mao may be useful before we continue our somewhat selective and fitful journey forward through Chinese cultural history. Mao, like all them godless commies, had a strong belief in the collective good over the personal good (I guess they never read the Gospel according to Wall Street—"Let ye who gets the most stuff be granted the glory of god"). Actually, it is probably more accurate to say that Communism in general, and the Maoist version in particular, views the collective good and the social good as one in the same—what is good for the society is good for me and what is good for me should be good for society. Mao once said,

> Our point of departure is to serve the people whole-heartedly and
> never for a moment divorce ourselves from the masses, to proceed
> in all cases from the interests of the people and not from one's
> self-interest or from the interests of a small group, and to identify
> our responsibility to the people with our responsibility to the
> leading organs of the Party.

This quote may leave a few of us American types scratching our heads wondering, "Uh, uh, uh, what's this whole responsibility for other people thing all about?" The Western political model is predicated upon inalienable rights such as life, liberty, the pursuit of happiness, and the right to buy 47 lbs boxes of cereal from Costco. As familiar as this idea is to us, it is as distant as it is from the majority of non-western political systems, including China. Were it not for a whole series of odd little historical accidents (Imagine twelfth-century news reports: "There was a huge multi horse pileup today outside of Jerusalem when a holy water cart collided with an olive vender keeping the crusaders stuck in traffic for up to 3 hours") Western political culture may have also come to place responsibility before rights. This is all to say that the Chinese understanding of political culture as it was influenced by Maoist Communism begins with a fundamentally different assumption than our own.

Even though Communism was first put forward by a German Jew who converted to Lutheranism and had a general disdain for the working classes and was further developed by Russian intellectuals who opposed all religious influence and did not understand the needs of their own people, it oddly has a nice affinity with Chinese culture (its sort of like Tom Cruise and Katie Holmes—they don't seem like they should go together but they do share scientology-induced bliss). The collective being primary over the individual, the spirit of cooperation and harmony over competition, as well as the devaluation of material wealth and a greater appreciation of the natural world are all present in both traditional Chinese religions as well as Maoist political thought. Part of this is, of course, conscious manipulation by that wily Mao to reshape communism to fit the Chinese tradition, but in another sense, this reshaping can only go so far. Certain cultures and political traditions seem to have no internal attraction to one another while others fit better than a mullet at a carnival. Or in the words of the sagacious creators of Sesame Street we must be able to recognize when "One of these things is not like the other, one of these things just doesn't belong."

I would not want anyone to think that if Confucius were alive during the twentieth century, he would be marching shoulder to shoulder with Stalin or Mao. Nor would Lao Tzu and the Buddha be going for tea with Marx or Lenin (as thoroughly amusing as that might be). To assert that there is an affinity between traditional Chinese culture and Communism, is not to suggest that they are fungible (what a great word) or that they parallel each other on every point. Rather, if we were to imagine all of these men in a room together they would agree on many points, but if we asked them why it would break down to a three-stoogesesque scene in which Mao would try to poke Lao Tzu in the eyes, Confucius would hit Mao with his walking stick, and the Buddha would just sit back rub his belly and laugh. In a sense, community, harmony, and simplicity are shared values with very different sources.

Community, harmony, and simplicity may be ideals of traditional Chinese culture and Maoist thought alike, but someone seems to have forgotten to tell the residents of Shanghai, Beijing, Nanjing, Hongzhou, or basically every other Chinese city about it. Perhaps its just me, but I have a very difficult time squaring Communism with the existence of shopping malls that are so glitzy that they would make the entire city of Beverly Hills get a collective facelift. It also seems a bit curious that in a country that, at one time, had a deep appreciation of the harmony of nature, you could develop asthma from simply breathing the air. And I am not quite sure how the Buddha would feel about people wearing Gucci and Prada while offering homage and prayer to the great Bodhisattvas (to be fair, Jesus was a fairly simple fellow as well and now some of his place of worship actually have their own Starbucks— "Hmmm . . . I think I will have a vente half calf mother Mary latte and some reduced fat communion wafers"). Modern Chinese cities are filled with shiny new buildings, designer shopping malls, and a growing middle class that love their electronic gadgets as much as us folks back in the good ol' US of A. It is almost as if in the Chinese desire to compete with America, they have actually become better capitalists than us.

We will pause here for a moment for all the antiglobalization activists to stand up and yell about the evils of Westernization, how America is ruining the world, and how Colonel Sanders, Ronald McDonald, and the little red-headed girl from Wendy's are all part of an evil cabal trying to take over the universe. Once they run out of breath from yelling, we can think back to the first chapter and remember that globalization does not equal Westernization and that what we see in modern-day China is not a corruption of Chinese culture, but rather just Chinese culture as it continues to evolve and change over time. While in China I had dinner with a friend who had been living there for over four years, and the conversation ended up about fast food restaurants. He pointed out that when the Chinese people go to McDonald's or KFC they do not view it as going to a Western or American restaurant, they just see it as food. The allure of these places is not their association with America or their symbolic representation of democracy and economic liberalism, but simply their oh so yummy French fries. The fact that contemporary Chinese culture is not necessarily a form or result of Westernization is also made fairly obvious to anyone who has ever read a Chinese newspaper (which are all state controlled and usually awkwardly worded in English, but all the more fun for this). A vast number of the editorials refer to the rise of China, the Chinese century, or the end of US dominance. This could of course be seen as government-sponsored propaganda (not nearly as much fun as the Mao stuff of the 60s and 70s), but even then it reflects a the consciousness of the people and culture. There is not so much a sense of trying to be like the United States as there is taking what works from the United States and making it Chinese (through cultural appropriation not through magic—poof, Chinese).

Modern China defies expectations. Whereas the average American may expect too see oppressed workers, bicycles, Communist propaganda, Buddhist temples, traditional Chinese dress, and Kung Fu fighting (well, the last one might have just been what I hoped to see), what you actually see are thoroughly if not hyper-modern cities, stylish young people, swift new trains, glittering shopping malls, and a population that seems far more hopeful than oppressed. This is a broad generalization since China is a very large country, and it would be like grouping together people from rural Mississippi and Detroit (a good time to be sure— I mean what could go wrong they both like guns). Despite how many differences there may be between different regions in China, as was mentioned in the first chapter, a network of family resemblances remains. In this case, behind the shiny veneer remains strong influence of both Communism and traditional Chinese culture/religion. Even as external elements of nations and cultures change, patterns of thought and consciousness remain influential. An example of this is that to the untrained eye America does not look like medieval Europe (or at least I haven't noticed many knights riding around or people dying from the plague), and yet the Christian cultural influences from that period remain alive and well today in our political arena. One of the traditional Christian objections to abortion is based upon the belief that at the moment of conception a fully formed, but very, very, small person appears in the mother's womb. While at the time, in the absence of medical science, this may have seemed plausible (I guess enough mead will make you believe anything), but even today when we have ultrasounds and we know the baby it is not hanging out in there playing frisbee, many people still hold to old religious and cultural ideas. While this may be an extreme example the point remains the same: Even as things change, previous cultural forms and patterns of thought remain powerfully influential in our encounter with the world.

All cultures, including our own, are riddled with contradictions and paradoxes (i.e., our television programs are filled with sexuality and yet we teach abstinence education. Conservatives oppose abortion yet support the death penalty. And we teach our children to not do drugs, then pump them full of anything and everything that a pharmacist will give us). The paradoxes in modern Chinese society may, however, not be as powerful or problematic as they either first appear or would be in America. Confucius teaches social harmony and the importance of familial relations, yet millions of young Chinese are moving away from home to make their way in the world. Lao Tzu teaches harmony and the value of nature, and yet China is one of the most polluted countries on Earth. The Buddha teaches simplicity, while modern Chinese youth look like they are straight out of an episode of Gossip Girl. To the Western mind, it may seem as though modernization has trampled traditional Chinese culture and values more thoroughly than a pilgrim in a Indian temple stampede, but remember this is in part because we do not much care for contradiction while it is less problematic in Chinese thought. While for us it may be old or new, modern or traditional, Communist or capitalist, chicken fingers or pizza, to the Chinese mindset the old and new, modern and traditional, and Communist and capitalist can coexist in harmony (apparently so can chicken fingers and pizza in the United States, where my wife's sister has a particular love for chicken-finger pizza—America is such a magical place). In the end, when we try to understand the culture and consciousness of modern China we should remember that it is not either-or, but rather both-and.

For as much as old and new cultural elements coexist within contemporary China, there does seem to be a bit a of a curious relationship to the past. It is almost as if one of the tenets of the Cultural Revolution outlived Mao and Maoism: out with the old and in with the new. Do not get me wrong, there are countless historic sights, national parks, temples, and museums (I have the pictures and empty wallet to prove it—many of these places are oddly and frustratingly expensive). It is no so much that the history has been paved over as we like to do here in America (we need more Dunkin Donuts in case the one in other strip mall has a line), but rather that it has become sort of quaint or passé. Whereas the philosophically problematic motto of your high school history teacher was, "Those who do not remember history are doomed to repeat it," the Chinese motto is, "Those who do not keep moving forward are doomed to repeat it." There is a frenetic sense of forward motion in modern China as if the past was chasing them like Wile E. Coyote hunting down the Road Runner, or Tom pursuing Jerry (I watched a few too many hours of cartoons as a child).

Notes

1. Chenglie, Luo. *A Collection of Confucius' Sayings*. Ji Nan: Qi Lu Press, 1988, p. 22.
2. Ibid.
3. Theodore De Barry, W. M. *Sources of the Chinese Tradition*. New York: Columbia University Press, 1960, pp. 49–50.
4. Chan, Wing-tsit. *The Way of Lao Tzu*. Prentice Hall, 1963, p. 97.
5. Ibid., p. 132.
6. Palmer, Martin, and Elizabeth Breuilly. *The Book of Chuang Tzu*. Penguin (Nonclassics), 1996, p. 108.
7. Nisbett, Richard. The Geography of Thought: How Asians and Westerners Think Differently . . . and Why. Free Press, 2004.
8. p. 132.
9. Nisbett, p. xx.

Suggestions for Further Reading

Confucius. *The Analects*. Oxford University Press, USA, 2008.
Fronsdal, Gil. *The Dhammapada: A New Translation of the Buddhist Classic with Annotations*. Shambhala, 2006.
Morton, W. Scott, Charlton M. Lewis, W. Scott Morton, and Charlton Lewis. *China: Its History and Culture*. 4th ed. McGraw-Hill, 2004.
Pan, Philip P. *Out of Mao's Shadow: The Struggle for the Soul of a New China*. Reprint. Simon & Schuster, 2009.
Sharma, Shalendra D. *China and India in the Age of Globalization*. 1st ed. Cambridge University Press, 2009.
Troost, J. Maarten. *Lost on Planet China: One Man's Attempt to Understand the World's Most Mystifying Nation*. Reprint. Broadway, 2009.
Tzu, Lao. *Tao Te Ching: A New English Version*. Harper Perennial Modern Classics, 2006.

4

(Not) Watching TV in China

Thank You for Watching Chinese Central Television (Not That You Have a Choice)

I know that I have been beginning each chapter with an exercise, but I think I am going to give you the chapter off. Your brain, much like your muscles, needs time to rest and recover. Actually, I am lying (not about the muscle recovery part). This entire chapter will in itself be an exercise, in the sense that it will be our first attempt at analyzing American television programming from a distinct cultural perspective. Since I have just taken you on a journey through China, it would seem the logical place to begin, although we could always defy logic and start discussing television in Djibouti (by far the best name of any country in the world). Leaving Djibouti aside, discussing and analyzing American television in China is a fascinating exercise that will help us gain insight into the construction and understanding of the American identity abroad as well as how this contributes to intercultural misunderstanding and communication.

Something interesting happened during my first trip to China as I was pursuing research on television. On my very first day after a hard-fought battle with asthma-inducing pollution, my realization that not speaking Chinese would hinder my ability to communicate (why I did not think of this before is a testament to my keen powers of foresight), and my warp-speed Disney monorail ride from the airport, I check into my hotel above the Starbucks and all I want to do is sit down, relax, and watch a little TV. After figuring out how to turn on the lights and overcoming my discomfort with finding a vibrating condom as one of the included toiletries (which of course was only made worse by the unsettling phone call I received at one in the morning offering me a "very best massage"—I really need to stay at nicer places), I deciphered the remote control and turned on the TV. The first station I encountered was in Chinese, as was the second, and the third, the fifteenth, and the twenty-seventh. Yes, every single station was in Chinese, and not one of them had any American programming. My response to this realization was one word uttered very loudly, which I will refrain from writing here, a synonym for *copulate* and rhymes with *duck*.

After my initial breakdown, both on account of my inability to do research and the fact that I would now be in China for weeks with no TV, I pulled myself together, bought a cheap bottle of scotch, and set about figuring out where I went wrong. The first place I went wrong was in not doing enough legwork (that whole foresight thing really is a problem). If I had been properly prepared I would have realized that while Cable TV is very common in China, to the point where they have the largest cable market in the world, which I suppose would make sense as they have the largest population in the world, the availability of American programming on TV is sort of like finding vegetarian food in the South—it is possible but the selection, availability, and quality are highly suspect (although I do love good fried green tomatoes). While the cable market may be vast, it is, like almost everything else in China, strictly controlled and supervised. It is possible to obtain a cable license that will allow you to receive international channels including HBO, CNN, but few Chinese citizens have this and even when they do the programming is more closely monitored than a child with ADHD in an antique store.

An interesting example of the, to put it politely, careful supervision of TV programming in China was relayed to me by a friend who has been living in Shanghai for the past 4 years. He was watching CNN during the run up to the Beijing Olympic Games during the time at which the protests were occurring in France and other countries with regard to the torch relay. Just as CNN began airing coverage of the events, the channel went black. It is troubling in itself that the government closely monitors every station to the point where they are able to block the station as soon as anything "controversial" is aired. I can just see a guy sitting there nervously with his hand over the button, beads of sweat forming on his forehead, as he anxiously waits for the first signs of any disturbing material, hoping that he does not wait a second too long and allow even an extra verb to escape from the mouths of those damn capitalists and imperialists over at CNN. What is perhaps equally troubling is that the station did not go down for the course of the one story alone, it did not reappear till a full day later. The censors were most likely waiting for the news cycle to move on to the next major story (maybe the military junta in Burma, or the Middle-East Crisis, or even more importantly, Brittney spears or Jessica Simpson getting fat) so as to not run the risk of contaminating the national consciousness.

Breaking the Law

So if I, and for that matter the majority of Chinese people, was not going to be able watch much American programming on TV, where was I going to find it (and perhaps more importantly, how was I going to explain to my editor that the entire premise of my book was a tad shaky). The answer came as I was on my way to dinner. Walking forlorn and dejected down the streets of Shanghai, I was confronted by a man who I thought was trying to sell me CDs, and, being no particular fan of Chinese pop music, I politely declined. When he insisted, after initially thinking that for once in my life I am bigger than everyone around me and I can be intimidating and then realizing that all 145 pounds of me was not going to scare anyone, I looked down at what he was offering and saw a curious sight, Rachel, Ross, Phoebe, Joey, Chandler, and Monica. He was trying to sell me bootlegged copies of Friends. My first response was, "I don't get it, did I go back in a time warp? Is it 1995? Someone didn't tell me." Of course since he spoke no English, this comment was returned with a blank stare. Along with the DVD's of *Friends*, were also copies of *Prison Break, CSI, Lost, 24, Gossip Girl,* and pretty much every other popular American television program of the last five years. After a bit of negotiation, well more like trying to figure out Chinese numbers and the currency conversion, and initially accidentally offering 23 cents, we settled on a price of $1.50. Yes folks, you can get the entire last season of Lost for less than the price of a cup of coffee (take that Christian Children's Fund).

Having scored enough bootleg TV to keep me entertained for the next few weeks, I returned to my hotel room with a spring in my step and considerably less fear that my editor would send the Triad after me.

When I got there, I thought that I would share the good news with my wife by sending her an e-mail (to which she later replied, "You're where? I thought you went out for coffee"). While online I realized that while the Chinese government could closely control TV, it would be far more difficult to control the entire Internet. And sure enough, after a bit of searching I was able to track down a few different Web sites that subtitled or dubbed current American programming into Chinese. These Web sites are occasionally shut down by the government for carrying "antisocial" content, but the government is too busy censoring major Web sites like Google and Yahoo to have much time for the little guys.[1] The Chinese government is currently working on techniques to further censor the Internet, including installing chips in all new computers that will block certain content, mainly pornography (because you know if you have continual riots in the Western regions of your country, massive poverty, major human rights abuses, and life-threatening pollution, porn is really what you should focus your energy and attention on).

As of right now, and it is growing exponentially by the day, roughly 200 million people in China have access to the Internet.[2] At least 65 million of these people are connected via high-speed lines of some form, a higher number than in the United States.[3] What this means is that the potential audience for American programming in China is enormous and growing—sort of like our national debt. Whereas on Chinese television all forms of programming have strict limits on the amount of sexuality and violence, which other than game shows (maybe that can have jeopardy contestants stand over a pool of sharks and be dropped if they get the question wrong—thereby actually placing them in jeopardy) is the makeup of American programming, the Internet has no such limits unless you get caught.[4] So while the majority American programming has no present or future on Chinese cable television, its presence is and will likely continue to be all over the Internet.

At some point, Internet censorship may well become a problem for Chinese viewers who are desperate to see the latest wacky time traveling mishaps of the people on the *Lost* island, or the next day the world is going to be destroyed on *Heroes*. That said, for as many techniques as the Chinese government comes up with to block antisocial content, there is always an inventive person who finds a way around it. I discovered this one day while I was trying to read the *Washington Post* online while staying in Nanjing. I was enjoying the latest neoconservative lambaste by Charles Krauthamer, when the page just froze. The entire site went down, and I could no longer access it. Thinking this was just a glitch, I tried other noncontroversial Web sites and they all loaded correctly. No *New York Times*, no *Washington Post*, no CNN, no major American news sources at all. Luckily the Chinese know as little about American geography as Americans and have no idea that *Des Moines* is even a place let alone as a newspaper, so I could access the *Des Moines Register*.

Besides learning all about corn from the *Des Moines Register* (big news in Iowa), I also discovered something else: circumventors. A circumventor is a web program that allows you to circumvent (surprise!) web blocking by accessing a site through a secondary site. It would be like not being able to fly directly to Cuba from New York, so instead you go through Montreal (not that I know anyone who has done this). By using a circumventor I, and, therefore, anyone in China with Internet access could get around the blocks on American news sites, antigovernment Web sites, media portals, and pornography (I only checked for research purposes). What this means is that try as they might, the Chinese government has a long way to go to block TV over the Internet.

After a few days of watching American programming on DVD and online, I barely even missed the warming glow of my 55-inch, widescreen, HD, LCD, 1080p, ABC, 123, Doe Re Me TV. In fact, the entire viewing experience changes—something that anyone who has ever sat down to watch an entire season of 24 on DVD in 24 hours can tell you (actually closer to 18 hours if you account for there not being any commercials, but then you still have to factor in bathroom breaks and time to answer the door and pay the pizza delivery guy, so it's a wash in the end). The fact that the majority of Chinese viewers of American television programming are watching it on either DVD or online, and thereby do not contend with commercials and are also able to control the timeframe and way in which they encounter the programs, is a fascinating point. The mode and medium of encounter changes the viewing experience itself. As interesting as a point as this is and as worthwhile as it may be to explore at another time (yet another book for me to write—hint, hint Continuum Press), it does not really affect our primary concern, which is the encounter of cultures and the meaning of the images. It is enough for now to recognize that while the Chinese government may be stricter than Mormon parents when it comes to what its people can watch on TV (although I seriously doubt that Joe Smith and Mao would have gotten along very well), the Chinese people still have significant access to American programming.

Mind-Numbing Goodness

We are going to shift our focus away from how people in China come to encounter American television programming and begin to examine what they encounter when they do sit down with the DVDs or in front of their computers. As was discussed in the first two chapters, there is no one Chinese television viewer. If we were to go interview Hu Jin Tao, a middle-class office worker in Shanghai, and a rural farmer in Sichuan province, we would clearly encounter distinct human beings, each with his own personal story, ideas, emotions, and quirks (I have heard that Hu Jin Tao is a huge fan of Chuck-E-Cheese's—well, maybe not, but who doesn't love a good game of whack-a-mole). While these differences are significant and contribute to our unique presence in the world, underneath of them we can still find a range of family resemblances that allow us to speak of a shared cultural horizon. Drawing upon some of the cultural elements discussed in the previous chapter, we will begin to look and see what cultural images and metaphors are being projected and received by some of the most popular American programming in China and how that influences the perception and understanding of the American identity. So get your favorite snack food (I am going with popcorn, but feel free to go with something more ethnically appropriate like shrimp chips), find that comfortable worn-out spot on the couch, and settle in for America's favorite pastime: sitting on our bums—sorry, I meant watching TV.

The choice of programs to analyze is broad, and each one would provide its own unique lens into the phenomenon of that we are trying to understand, but much like modes of transportation some are just better than others (I am currently trying to write while sitting on a bus, so my vote—and as the author mine is the only one that counts—is to put busses at the bottom of the list). The relative adequacy of programs for our little endeavor is not about their inherent quality (although it would be funny to put Masterpiece Theater up against The Real Housewives of New Jersey), but rather their popularity among Chinese audiences as well as their capacity to open up comparative cultural horizons. Or to put this in other terms for those not fluent in academes, we want shows that give us a lot of interesting stuff to talk about and that people like to watch. To this end, I have decided on three shows, *Friends*, *Prison Break*, and *Lost*, which at first glance make no sense together. But worry not, on second glance, they still make no sense together—but they make perfect sense individually.

Friends

Upon hearing that we are going to be discussing *Friends*, I will assume that your response was something akin to mine when the charmingly persistent fellow in Shanghai tried to sell me the DVDs, "Yeah, let me just run our and get the Rachel haircut, pull out my flannel shirt, and dust off my Spice Girls tape, to get me in the right time frame." Do not get me wrong here, I know there are some people who are still devoted fans of *Friends* and can quote every episode line for line (there are places to get help for that), but it does seem a bit curious that it would be or remain so popular in China. When *Friends* originally started airing back in 1994 China was a very different place (as was the United States, to be fair, but having slightly better hairstyles and fashion does not quite compare with vast economic and technological development).

When we think of *Friends*, what probably comes to mind is a somewhat amusing sitcom about a bunch of quasi socially dysfunctional, Gen X New Yorkers, who more or less share the same psychological, emotional, and social maladies as their generation—and thereby much of the American population. As we watch *Friends*, we are very much watching ourselves. We are watching our own friendship network, our own failed relationships, our own quirky or womanizing friends, and our own general struggles with our careers, families, and life-course decisions. Perhaps our crises are not quite as exaggerated or amusing as those on the show (or at least I would hope not), but there is a degree of resonance and familiarity. Being of the same generation and cultural background of the creators of the show places us largely within a shared lifeworld that draws upon a set of common cultural metaphors and similar sense of the American identity. In the case of *Friends*, this has much to do with out relationship to our (wait for it, wait for it) friends. Yes, all of those years spent getting a PhD makes me a master of the obvious.

There has been a general shift in our own sense of ourselves over the past generation, which has moved us away from the traditional cohesive sense of identity to one far more dependent upon context, social networks, and our friends rather than our family or community. All of you currently checking your Facebook status as you are reading this book know exactly what I am talking about (yeah, I know you are doing it, and I find it incredibly impolite). To watch *Friends* as an American is, then, to see a reflection of our own cultural sense of ourselves as fluid and somewhat socially dislocated from any firm and singular base of identity.

The average Chinese viewer would encounter something very different from us socially dislocated Americans when they watch friends. They would see Confucius. I do not mean this literally of course, although it would be quite amusing to have the old guy sitting around in the coffee shop with the gang writing pithy little statements on slips of paper ("Confucius say: He who is on a break should be careful of which bed he lies in"—a joke for all you diehard fans). The cultural metaphors being projected and reflected from *Friends* in China are based upon the Chinese cultural traditions, and in this case if we think back to the last chapter (I know it was a while ago) you may recall the centrality of networks of relationships. If we were to begin with the Chinese cultural metaphors of the social coming before the personal and our being defined by our networks of relationships, then the images encountered in *Friends* take on a whole new meaning. To the Chinese viewer Ross, Rachel, and the gang are not desperately seeking some kind of solidity and sense of self through the other due to a lack of a sense of personal meaning or purpose, they are always defined, and find meaning, in and through the other. This idea, which would horrify any good red-blooded American who has been taught that independence is more important than even truth, justice, or McDonald's, is so much a part of the Chinese cultural world both in terms of the Confucian tradition as well as the Communist ideology that to watch *Friends* is to see it clearly represented.

Another example will help to clarify the distinct understandings of relationships that are present in *Friends*. The character of Joey was portrayed as a womanizer for much of the show, and while never shown as dirty or creepy, it was clear that he would not have stood up to Republican law makers moral standards (at least the ones they espouse, he would fit nicely with the ones they actually practice). This character plays upon an American conception of male sexuality and relational capabilities (or I suppose lack thereof), while drawing upon the cultural trend toward a loss of fidelity and commitment in relationships, forgoing the final couple of seasons with regard to Rachel. To us, Joey's philandering is representative of an inability to form close bonds and engage in loving romantic relationships. But then, our country was founded by a bunch of religious zealots with a very strict sexual morality (I love how the pilgrims are always portrayed to children as these happy folks seeking freedom—which I suppose is easier than trying to explain to kids that our country was started by a bunch of religious wonks who were so uncompromising in their beliefs they were basically thrown out of their own country). The Chinese, however, have no happy pilgrims to beset them with a puritanical attitude toward sexuality. In fact, there is a rapidly growing number of abortions among teenagers in China, in part due to the lack of taboo toward sexuality that is leading many friends to engage in casual sexual relationships, along with a complete and total lack of sexual education (lesson to be learned: sexual liberalism good, not using a condom bad). Regardless of moral reaction, what this means in terms of television viewing is that the average Chinese youth watching *Friends* would not necessarily see Joey as a womanizer or as an American who is incapable of engaging in positive romantic relationships. Interestingly, in the end they may well see us in a far more positive light than we do.

One more interestingly multivocal element in *Friends*, at least until the final season when Chandler and Monica buy the house, is the use of space and living arrangements. The group of friends is continually either in Monica's apartment, which in turn inherited from her grandmother in order to maintain rent control (a point of significant jealousy for me as a resident of New York, spending half my salary to live in a place that is so small that I can cook and shower at the same time—convenient to be sure, but potentially dangerous when I use the toaster), or in a coffee shop, in which various people have worked at different points. They have also shifted and rearranged living arrangements countless times, with the result being a reshuffling of what appears almost to be common space. Occasionally, we find them in different locations, but certainly never alone, not for long, and we can be sure they will soon return to their shared space. From our perspective, these are just people trying to get by economically and doing what is necessary to live in a major city in the United States. From a Chinese perspective, however, with the cultural emphasis on harmony and the political emphasis on Communism, this begins to look a whole lot like socialism (shhh . . . don't tell the Republicans they may try to ban the reruns). While each may have their own jobs, they tend to work for the social good, live in shared space, and help to support each other both emotionally and economically. So again, what to us may appear to be people struggling financially and having to be creative in order to live the American dream may have a far more positive reading from a Chinese perspective. In many ways the cultural metaphors in place for the average Chinese person will manifest in an understanding of the program that makes the Americans look cooperative, hardworking, and concerned with the collective good, which would be sort of like looking at a bag of White Castle burgers and calling it health food.

Friends is such a fascinating show to consider in part because when we watch it in an everyday kind of way (TV in the background, texting someone, checking e-mail, eating popcorn, talking to the person next to us, crocheting sweaters for your pet Chihuahua) it seems completely benign. But when we begin to watch it with a degree of cultural awareness, or just simply any kind of awareness, we begin to encounter a very different program. From an American perspective we encounter a vision of ourselves as socially dislocated and dysfunctional, somewhat morally questionable, and in many ways struggling to get by. The Chinese variant of this, which is not colored by our cultural metaphors of despair and the decay of Western society (we are a cheery lot), is a vision of Americans as socially intertwined, engaged in healthy relationships, and almost socialist in their orientation. If *Friends* can be this multivocal, just imagine what happens when we encounter shows that are far more complicated. Okay, you can stop imagining because we are going to move on.

Prison Break

Taking a significant leap in every conceivable way (if you are going to go, go big—how American of me), we are going to shift our focus from *Friends* to *Prison Break*. Like I mentioned earlier, there really is no internal logic that connects the programs I chose to consider, which is made fairly obvious by my choice of putting *Friends* and *Prison Break* together in the same sentence. Whereas one is a good-natured sitcom whose maximum intensity comes in the form of Rachel's picking Ross or Joey, the other is a nail-biting ride where violence, murder, and intrigue are about as commonplace as water boarding at a CIA prison (great! Now my phones are going to be tapped). These two shows share nothing in terms of genre, format, character types, themes, issues, or, at least in the United States, audience. Even though there is no internal connection between these programs they are both wildly popular in China. It is like a vegetarian eating at steak house, a lover of classical music busting out rhymes at an MC battle, or Sarah Palin working as a receptionist at an abortion clinic (I could just hear her now: "Well, ya know I do support the death penalty, so I thought to myself we could just get it right out of the way and kill um sooner.") This seeming contradiction is an excellent place to begin.

For those who are unfamiliar with *Prison Break*, it is a show based upon the idea of someone being wrongfully incarcerated and his brother's attempt to save him—at least that is how it started in the first season (I assumed familiarity with *Friends* because if you been alive in the past decade and not in a cave or hulled up in a Unabomber shack in the woods the entire time, you have seen at least one episode). The show plays off themes of corruption in the government and justice system, the harsh reality of American prisons, and the vicious nature of both the criminals in the prisons, the people guarding them, as well as the lawmakers who are supposed to be looking out for the good of the people and nation. Overall, the picture it paints of America is enough to make us want to consider undoing the revolution and give ourselves back to Britain. Our society is shown as corrupt, dangerous, selfish, angry, and violent, at least to Americans. We are so predisposed to these cultural metaphors from our news sources and other television programs and movies that they just resonate with us. If, however, you begin from a different set of metaphors you get a very different image. Not that I have ever been, and hope that I will never have the occasion to be, to a Chinese prison, from what I understand they are not particularly pleasant places. There are frequent claims of torture and abuse, and often those who find themselves there will never see the outside again. There have been reports of Chinese police using "a range of punishments that leave no physical bruises and thus may not be illegal under Chinese law."[5] I am not quite sure what this means, but it is certain that if most people were offered a choice between that and a day at Disneyworld they would probably choose Disneyworld (except maybe my wife who has an un-American disdain for the happiest place on Earth). Whereas the jail in *Prison Break* may seem bad to us, they do get food, time to go outside, access to legal representation, and basic health care. I am not saying that the American prison system is good (in fact, we have a greater percentage of our population incarcerated than any other country, including China), but if the Chinese system is a Motel Six, than the American system is the Ritz Carlton by comparison. If you add to this conundrum an all pervasive government corruption and a justice system that really should put the word "justice" in quotation marks to show that it is more of a suggestion, a very different set of cultural metaphors begin to emerge that would lead to a distinct encounter of the program. This understanding of *Prison Break* is one in which justice is a real possibility and the wrongfully accused may actually have a chance.

Another striking aspect of *Prison Break* is its moral ambiguity. There are the good characters that we cheer for and want to escape (over and over again), and there are the bad guys, who have little to no redeeming qualities. But there are also the not actually good guys, who we sort of need to cheer for, because they are helping the good guys, but we also sometimes do not like, because they have done bad things, and do not really trust because we know they might betray the good guys. For those who have seen the show, this makes perfect sense; for everyone else, well, you get the idea. As Americans we want justice to be done and good to triumph (you can insert a bit of ironic laughter here). Perhaps I should have said that in spite of our somewhat questionable ethical record on the international stage over the past 10, no 20, no 50 years, Americans like most of those under the sway of Judeo-Christian morality tend toward dialectical thinking. When we watch *Prison Break* we want Michael and Lincoln to succeed and the Company to fail. One is good, one is bad, and there is nothing in between.

As was discussed in the previous chapter, the type of dialectical thinking and categorical morality that is present in the West is not present in East Asian thought. For a show like *Prison Break*, this becomes particularly fascinating because of the complexity and nuance of the characters and ethical dilemmas. Unlike the Republican view of other countries, few of the characters are either all good or all bad. Even Lincoln who was wrongly imprisoned for the murder of the vice-president's brother is still a criminal; he just happens to be in prison for the wrong crime. These complex characters that are not good or bad, but rather good and bad, fit nicely within the Chinese tradition that see light and dark as interpenetrating. Like the yin–yang symbol with its roots in Taoism and its tendency to be draped around the necks of teenagers who have no idea what it means, except for the fact that it is not Christian, shows there is always a balance between two opposing forces. In this light, the idea that we need to root for the good guy becomes secondary to the subtle interplay of forces that are present in people's lives. In this way, the show takes on a different coloring and becomes less about the escaping and the action and more about the characters.

To watch *Prison Break* in China is to encounter a program that in many ways resonates with both the contemporary political situation as well as the collective cultural inheritances. Therefore, whereas to us it is an adrenaline-filled hour that we can watch with guilty pleasure as we witness exactly how derelict and decayed our culture has become (and we do all love a good train wreck), to the Chinese audience, the situation appears quite different. The view of America is one that shows a country with significant problems but also one in which justice, truth, and freedom are all real possibilities. While the view of Americans, instead of being moralistic cowboys out to save/conquer the world as is often portrayed in the news, is one of subtlety and complexity. Perhaps Americans are not only good or bad but can also be good and bad. So again, what we find here is a fascinating example of how competing cultural metaphors placed upon a multivocal image leads to distinct understandings of America and Americans.

Lost

Just in case you are not yet confused enough, lets spend a bit of time discussing the most interesting, engaging, confusing, frustrating, nonsensical collage of philosophical, cultural, and religious ideas, which in no way go together and yet somehow still draw you in, on TV in recent years: *Lost*. For those unfamiliar with the show, it is ostensibly about a group of people who survived a plane crash and ended up on a mysterious island and their multiple attempts to escape, return, travel through time, unravel mysteries, uncover secret organizations, fight off smoke monsters, discover secret temples, evade polar bears (not making this up), and come to terms with their pasts, present, and future. If this does not sound strange enough, as the show has progressed it has taken on a more and more religious air, combining aspects of Judaism, Christianity, mythology, ancient Egyptian religions, and a touch of Buddhism and Hinduism into a sort of postmodern spiritual wonderland. I would make up some witty remark at this point about a biblical patriarch and an Egyptian god hanging out together, but I do not have to, since, at the end of the fifth season, the shows' creators did it for me by having the character Jacob living in a statue of the Egyptian god Anubis (I do not appreciate them stealing my comedic thunder).

For all of its oddities, absurdities, and curiosity, or perhaps because of all these things, *Lost* has an almost cult-like following in the United States. The cafeteria where I teach even has a *Lost* table the day after the show airs, where people can sit together and hypothesize over the latest ways in which the show has disobeyed the laws of physics (I personally avoid this meet-up, in large measure because I avoid the cafeteria as a whole—someone needs to inform catering that vegetarians do no only eat salads). A large measure of its popularity to American audiences is probably due to its use of mystery. In a disenchanted and cynical society (not me of course), where for all of the concern over the rise of evangelicalism, reason, and science still rule the day, a little awe and wonder can go a long way—and *Lost* has awe and wonder in spades. There is something wonderfully fantastical about *Lost* that entices viewers away from the banality and averageness of their big box store–shopping, chain restaurant–eating, cookie cutter house–living suburban wasteland (not that I have anything against the suburbs—clearly). For as wacky and nonsensical as it is, it at least has the feeling of depth and meaning. If you throw in the sense of purpose, togetherness, and a degree of excitement and energy found on the show, you basically have a corrective for everything every critic has said about America for the past 50 years. It is to the point where a good number of people would happily trade in their lives for a place on the island. In fact, I was recently on a plane to Japan with a group of students when I heard them eagerly discussing the possibility that the plane could crash on the *Lost* island. As disturbing as this was in numerous ways, I did get a nice ego boost when I overheard them say that I would "totally be like Jack."

The average Chinese viewer brings none of the suburban malaise, feeling of meaninglessness, or lack of community to their experience of *Lost*—these are the wonderful inheritances of American culture. For that matter, they also do not recognize the majority of the references to Jewish, Christian, or Egyptian themes. To be fair, the average American viewer gets few of these either (I once asked my students who remember the story of Adam and Eve, and the best they could come up with is that it had something to do with naked people, a snake, and an apple), but the references, even if not explicitly recalled, are embedded in our culture and consciousness. Without the ideas of cultural decay or cultural collage at play, as they are for American audiences, the Chinese viewer must be encountering something else when they watch Lost that resonates with their culture. To understand what this is all about, we need to spend some time with two of our friends from the last chapter, Lao Tzu (who didn't exist), and Mao (who many people wish hadn't existed).

In the previous chapter we discussed how the Taoist tradition following the imaginary Lao Tzu placed a strong emphasis on harmony, and particularly harmony with nature. While this may seem a tad ironic in light of modern China's massive problem with pollution, the idea of the veneration of nature still holds. Throughout *Lost*, we encounter various examples of people (John Locke) or peoples (the Others) attending to what the Island wants and trying to live in harmony with the island. It is as though the Island is itself a life force and that through bringing yourself in line with that force, you can lead a better, happier, easier, or at least somewhat less disastrous life. Images of the need for harmony with the island and with nature are present in multiple aspects of the show and can even be seen in the conflict between the Dharma Initiative who use technology and live in cute little suburban-looking houses and the Others who, at least first, lived in huts in the woods. While this is an important theme, it is clearly in itself not enough to explain the popularity. If what all Chinese viewers wanted to see was harmony with nature, it would be far less confusing to just watch *Animal Planet*—that is one, and maybe the only thing, I did not see bootleg DVDs of in China.

If we really want to understand the popularity of *Lost* in China, all we need to do is look at the title of the third episode of the first season, "Tabula Rasa." For those of you who slept through your Western civilization class, the title refers to an idea from John Locke (the philosopher, not the character on the show) that we are all born as blank slates. Throughout each of the seasons, *Lost* continually plays on this idea of starting over, having the past washed away, re-creation, going through the looking glass (another episode name) and coming out the other side, and also the meaning of time in general (hence, all the time traveling). While Mao may have carried it a bit further than the creators of *Lost*, as we discussed in the last chapter, he had a deep concern with progress (at least by his measure that seemed to include the killing and imprisonment of teachers, authors, and artists—I wouldn't have fared so well) and moving forward that has carried into the contemporary Chinese government and culture's mild obsession with paving/building/ toppling over of everything from the past. The possibility of being able to start all over again has strong appeal to a people, culture, and country in transition, and is something represented time and again in *Lost*.

Through a consideration of *Lost*, what we arrive at, other than a headache, is yet another picture of how America and the American identity is distinctly encountered by a Chinese audience. Rather than mystery, meaninglessness, and cultural confusion, the Chinese viewer through their cultural lens arrives at something closer to a show about nature, harmony, and the capacity for human and social transformation. This is not to say that all of these other images get ignored, although it would be funny if every time the smoke monster appeared everyone in China covered their eyes and pretended that is was not there. Of course, they see images of violence, the conflict, and the strife, but the meaning and implication of these images are read through a distinct set of cultural metaphors and inheritances that make *Lost* seem more like a show about

Tao and Mao than the breakdown of American culture (and it sounds better too). After looking at all three shows we can return to the point we began with: They share nothing in common. Well, there is one important exception; they are popular with both American and Chinese audiences. If their popularity cannot be attributed to their common genre, format, themes, character types, trend-setting hairstyles, charming portrayal of prison life, or mind-numbing, time-traveling, laws of physics–defying plot twists, then there must be something else that allows them to cross cultural boundaries. As we have seen, what each of these shows offers is a multivocal set of images that can be encountered, engaged, interpreted, and understood through distinct cultural lenses. If we think back to Chapter 1 when we discussed globalization and culture, this begins to make perfect sense (Ah yes! It's all coming together). If globalization is understood as the lived experience of people in the contemporary world relative to their geographical, cultural, and economic position, and culture is something that is primarily experienced in a nonreflexive way, structures our encounter with the world, and is simultaneously shared and open to limitless variety, creativity, and personal interpretation, then the fact that these programs can make sense to, and be popular, with Chinese and American audiences makes perfect sense. These programs are not imposed upon China through globalization; they are encountered as part of an inherently global world, in a way that is largely nonreflective and nonproblematic. What academics and others tend to forget is that for the most part people just live their lives without thinking about what they are doing (a point that should be resoundingly clear whenever you see someone stand in line at a Starbucks for 15 minutes only to get to the front of the line and say, "Oh, jeez, you know I don't know what I want."). Similarly when Americans, Chinese, or anyone else watch TV, they are for the most part just watching TV. But we will return to this point in Chapter 7.

Before I hop on a plane to India to give you a tour of the land of Delhi, dharma, and dysentery, let's first try to put together some of the images of the American identity we encountered in *Friends*, *Prison Break*, and *Lost*. On the American side, we end up with a picture of ourselves that includes our social dislocation, meaninglessness, disillusionment, injustice, and overarching craptacularness (yes, I am well aware this is not a word, but it really ought to be) as both individuals and as a culture. The Chinese picture is quite different. From this perspective, we end up with social integration, complex moral actors, and a sense of harmony with nature. What is so fascinating here is that it is as though we were actually watching completely distinct shows, and perhaps in one sense we are. When we begin with distinct cultural backgrounds we end up encountering distinctly different worlds, but as we will discuss in Chapter 8, this actually opens a space for deep and penetrating (funny imagery) intercultural communication. But before we can get there, I need to take you on a trip through the subcontinent. So, I am off to the pharmacy to buy some Imodium, pick up my dhoti from dry cleaner, wrap myself in beads, douse myself in bug spray, and pick up 47 magazines for the 14-hour flight. See you on the other side.

Notes

1. "Chinese Fans Follow American TV Online — for Free: NPR." http://www.npr.org/

2. Ibid.

3. "China Overtaking US for Fast Internet Access as Africa Gets Left Behind," http://www.guardian.co.uk

4. French, Howard W. "Chinese Tech Buffs Slake Thirst for U.S. TV Shows." http://www.nytimes.com/2006/08/09/world/asia/09china.html.

5. Pan, Philip P. "Abuse Found in China Prisons." *The Washington Post*, December 3, 2005.

5

A Passage to India

Exercise #4

Once again you need to stop reading this book (after you finish the initial directions). What you need to do is track down an Indian video store, or you can use Netflix if you prefer. I would suggest the video store since if you find one it may also be near an Indian market and that way you can get some oh so yummy India snack food to go with the movie (personally I am a fan of the chakri, peanut bhaji, Bombay Chana, and the boondi masala—but you could always just eat popcorn with curry powder if you want to split the cultural difference). Once at the video store, rent any popular Bollywod movie—just ask the salesperson, I am sure that he will be very, very, happy to help.

(Just writing about the snacks made me hungry, so I am also going to the market until you get back)

Snacks in hand and hips ready to gyrate, you should watch the movie from start to finish. Some of you may at first feel as though this is some form of punishment, but give it some time the musical stylings may actually grow on you. I can speak from personal experience on this one. I spent about three wonderful days sick in bed in an Indian hotel with nothing else to do but watch Bollywood movies—by the end, I was about ready to give up my career in education and become the next great Bollywood star. You may not want to hop the next flight to Mumbai, but at least give the film a chance.

(I am going out for more snack food)

Now, stop dancing for a little while (don't be embarrassed everyone else was getting into it also) and write down your reactions. What was your impression of the visuals and costumes? What did you think about the interactions between the characters? Were you able to pick up on the major themes and issues? What was your favorite dance number (this is probably less important)? Take time to really think about what you just saw, and take note of both your reactions as well as the questions you may have about what you did not understand.

(I think I overdid the snack food—I am going out for a walk)

What kind of language did you use to describe what you just saw? Did words like strange, curious, weird, odd, unusual, or bizarre find their way into your comments (or perhaps you just went with the more direct, "What the hell was that?") Did you pick up on the subtle social cues, mores, customs, traditions, and patterns of interaction that are present within Indian society? In the end, did you see a bunch of people dancing on the screen or did you watch a Bollywood movie? What is the difference?

(Dis)orientation

Welcome to India. I am very, nay absurdly, jetlagged. I think it may be three days before tomorrow, or perhaps it is a week ago, Thursday, or maybe it could be Easter so I could get some Cadbury Crème Eggs since I am very hungry. In any case, it is nice to once again have my feet on the ground in the land of Gandhi and Ganesha, and once I make it through the security check after the guard talks to me for 2 to 3 hours; try to avoid the various touts, tricksters, and con men, all trying to convince me they have the best hotel ever and that mine burned down; yell at the cab driver that I know the prepaid-taxi scam; survive traffic that would make NASCAR drivers tremble in fear; and politely inform the woman threatening to throw her baby at me that I will just let it fall to the ground, I can check into my room and pass out for a couple of days.

Before I am able to check into my hotel room I am swarmed by a horde of men dressed in saffron t-shirts and dhotis (imagine the Gandhi loin cloth) with pictures of Siva on them, walking barefoot down the street carrying giant poles decorated with what appears to be tinsel and pipe cleaner. Remembering from my swim classes from when I was a child that it is better not to fight a rip current, I decide to just relax and allow myself to by swept along by the chanting wave of men. After some amused glances on both sides, I decide to ask what exactly I am caught up in. It turns out that these men are on a 250-mile pilgrimage in honor of Lord Siva the destroyer (don't worry destruction is not viewed as a negative in the Hindu tradition since it is necessary for creation to begin anew—I do love cyclical time). Since I do not really feel quite up to so significant a spiritual journey at this moment, I finally edge my way to the side of the crowd and find myself standing in front of a row of buildings that appear to have been constructed of left-over bricks, tarps, and a few pieces of old rope. Just behind these ramshackle buildings, and an assortment of a cow, a goat, 473 motorcycles, a 7-foot high pile of trash, a small temple, and a stand selling what I am pretty sure are tastiest samosas I have ever had, is a shiny new mall surrounded by scaffolding made out of bamboo and twine. While I love contradiction, irony, and absurdity as much as anyone raised in the post–generation x era, this is pushing the limits even for me.

If China is a curious place, than India is something like being at Disney World on psychedelic drugs (not that I would know this from personal experience). Modern India is a country of 1.1 billion people compressed into a space about one third the size of the United States. So if we do the basic math (and that is about all I can handle), we arrive at a picture of a country with 12 times greater population density than our own great nation. The cities of Mumbai and New Delhi alone have more people than the entire country of Canada (but Canada clearly wins out in terms of beavers, maple syrup, and angry francophones). Economically, India is one of the fastest growing economies with numerous businessmen ranking among the wealthiest in the world, and yet 20 percent of the population lives on less than 20 rupees (50 cents) a day. It is a secular democracy, but has devoutly religious Hindu and Muslim populations (your fun Jeopardy fact of the day is that it actually has the second largest number of Muslims of any country in the world after Indonesia). India is rapidly modernizing, and yet large numbers of the population live without electricity or running water. And let us not forget that it is the land of the Buddha, Gandhi, and the home in exile to the Dalai Lama, and is currently spending tens of billions of dollars to expand and modernize its army. But then any country with 10,000 gods is bound to have at least a few contradictions.

India's cultures and religions date back more than 3000 years and exhibit the influence of both indigenous traditions as well as those of the parade of traders, colonizers, and invaders who have interacted with the subcontinent over the generations. The greatest landmark/tourist trap in all of India is a relic of the days of Mogul rule (while worth visiting, the Taj Mahal is not quite all it is cracked up to be—with the countless touts and tricksters offering to sell you everything from Taj Mahal snow globes to the Taj Mahal itself, along with ticket prices that are 15 times higher for foreigners than for Indians, and the wild dogs that roam freely around the complex making the concern over getting rabies slightly higher than the marvel at the magnificence of the building, the experience goes from awe inspiring to absurdist rather quickly). The influence of the Raj can still readily be seen in everything from government buildings to the overly formal variant of English used by many Indians (Hotel clerk: "May I please have your good name sir?" Me: "Uhhh . . . . " Hotel Clerk: "Pardon me sir, Is there some difficulty?" Me: "Uhhh . . Do I have a good name?") There are Chinese fishing nets hanging in the coastal cities of Kerala, Dutch churches in Goa, and synagogues in Kolkata—albeit there are only about seven Jews left. All of this is to say that as was mentioned in the first chapter, globalization is not something new, but rather something that has always been, and India is the prime example of this.

Just to make the situation a bit more confusing, we should add in the fact that there are no less than 17 official languages spoken in India, some of which are from distinct language families that have absolutely no relation to one another. I actually met a woman on a train who was from the state of Karnataka in India where the language spoken is Kannada, while her husband was from Kerala where the spoken language is Malayalam. Neither husband nor wife spoke the others language (a problem that seems to exist even among people who do share the same language) so they could only communicate with each other in English. Oh, and to make it funnier, they were living in Qatar and yet neither spoke any Arabic (I think they just started drawing pictures and using smoke signals). While we Americans may see all them Indians as the same (you know, brown skin, funny accent, smells like curry, red dot on the forehead, works at a quickie mart), there is actually significant cultural, ethnic, religious, and socioeconomic diversity—so much so in fact that a man from Kerala who was living in New York once told me that his mother would rather have him marry a White Christian than someone from Northern India. It is good to know that we are not the only ones who embrace blind racism and prejudice.

If it is true that India is a country of deep contradiction, unpredictability, and diverse influences, then making any kind of inclusive comments about its culture would seem more difficult than getting a politician to answer a questions directly. While no one thing may apply to all Indians, as was mentioned in chapter 1 and as we saw in chapter 3. . . there are family resemblances and webs of connection that allow us to get a sense of a culture. India like China, and even our own great country of patriotic hillbillies and blue-state anti-American communists, is simultaneously infinitely varied and oddly singular. To this end, through exploring a few significant aspects of Indian history, culture, and religion, we may be able to begin to get a sense of this nation of chaos and inner peace through yoga, Ayurveda, and artery-clogging deep-fried foods; Buddha and modern-day banditry in the place where he attained enlightenment; and Gandhi and the Agni, a long-range ballistic missile.

This God Is Your God, This god Is My God, from Varanasi to the Bay of Bengal . . .

If we are going to begin to get a sense of modern India we need to turn to Brahma, since according to the Hindu tradition he is the god that brings the world into being. Recognizing the difficulty in communicating with divine, perhaps we would be better off starting with the religion that believes in Brahma. Hinduism is certainly not the only religion in India (remember your Jeopardy fact from before?), but it is by far the most influential, and most pervasive; it is the origin of Buddhism, Jainism, and Sikhism, and it shares much in common with these three other faiths as well. India is a Hindu-majority land, and while technically a secular democracy, the religious and cultural influence of Hinduism can be felt throughout the country. It is sort of like America and Christianity; we are technically a secular country, but the way we structure our society still strongly reflects a Judeo-Christian worldview (i.e., antisodomy laws, brothel laws, the debate over abortion, not being able to buy liquor in some parts of the country on Sunday, and the impossibility of getting into a Cracker Barrel on a Sunday morning—although I am not quite sure why you would want to anyway). The problem with trying to discuss Hinduism is that it is more difficult to define than pornography (but I know it if I see it—extra credit points if you get the reference).

Arvind Sharma, an eminent yet quirky scholar of Hinduism (in one of his classes at McGill University, in which I was enrolled, he actually said, "I do not much like grading, I always end up getting into trouble with it. So, we will only have one test half way through the class." He then proceeded to give one person an A and everyone else A minuses—you will have to guess which grade I received), once wrote that " . . . one is most a Hindu when least a Hindu, that is, when one has dissolved one's Hindu particularity in Hinduism all-embracing inclusiveness."[1] This Yoda-worthy statement is shortly followed by another in which he claims that "Fundamentally a Hindu may be identified as one who does not deny being one."[2] These amusingly cryptic, but not particularly enlightening remarks, do speak to something significant within the Hindu tradition: its inability to be easily defined is due in part to it inclusiveness and universality. This attitude is reflected in the first cab ride I ever took in India, in which the driver had statues of Vishnu (the god of preservation), Ganesha (the god of protection), Guru Nanak (the founder of Sikhism), a rosary, and a Jewish star on his dashboard. When I inquired about his collection he simply replied, "I am a Hindu. If it is god it is good."

While Hinduism may be a fairly inclusive and universalist religion, it does have a guiding idea of the nature and order of the world. On of the central principles of Hinduism is dharma, something that can be translated in various ways, but generally has the connotation of duty/responsibility. While us Westerners may recoil at the idea of duty or responsibility, preferring leisure, gluttony, and excess whenever possible (I am starting to think that we may soon hire people to even go to the bathroom for us—though I am not quite sure how this will work), the sense of duty conveyed by the word dharma relates to an entire worldview that is only meaningful within a larger frame. Duty in this sense is not a singular act like being responsible for taking the trash out, or even a set of actions, like taking the trash out, washing the windows, and mowing the lawn (I don't do bathrooms). Rather than duty relating to action, it relates to—and here we get to get all deep and philosophical— the being of our being. Dharma or duty is primarily about the kind of person that you are, and the actions follow from this. To put this in language that will wake you from your theological coma, teaching classes, making lesson plans, grading papers, and finding ways to torment students does not make me a teacher; rather, because I am a teacher I do all of those things. This may seem like a small distinction, but it is one that has a profound affect on consciousness. In many ways the being before doing orientation is not as common to the West, and this is part of the reason that we experience many of the things we do as a burden. If I tell you to do your homework, you will pout, stamp your feet, and slam the door to your bedroom. If, however, you know yourself to be a student, then you do your homework as an aspect of who you are (though this is admittedly uncommon).

This idea of dharma finds no better expression than in the Hindu scripture the Bhagavad Gita. The Gita, which is part of the great Indian epic the Mahabharata (which is repetitive since it basically translates into "great India" epic) is one of the most widely read and influential scriptures in the Hindu canon (in the literary sense, not in the weaponry sense). Even though there are countless scriptures in the Hindu tradition, we could almost consider it the Hindu Bible, except unlike the Bible, people actually read it and follow its teachings, and do not simply use it as a source of oppression, hatred, or political manipulation. The Gita is basically a long discussion between the Hindu god Krishna (who is himself an incarnation of Vishnu, who is a manifestation of Ishvara, which is itself a qualified form of Brahman—I will enroll you in an intro to Eastern religions course when you finish the book) and Arjuna, who is a great warrior about to enter into battle. As the story goes, Arjuna is surveying the battlefield, sees friends and family on the opposing side, and realizes that he cannot go to war and kill these fellow men whom he deems worthy of respect. Now, where we hippie types may view Arjuna's realization full of love, respect, and peace, that old trickster Krishna basically laughs at him and calls him a pansy, using slightly more pro- found language of course. Krishna suggest that Arjuna is not making some great gesture toward peace but rather misunderstanding the nature of the world. Krishna remarks that "Actions are all effected by the qualities of nature; but deluded by individuality the self thinks, 'I am the Actor.'"[3] This is a bit of a tricky one for the lovers of control and masters-of-our-own-destiny types to grasp, but Krishna is basically suggesting that our actions are not our own, we just wrongly believe that they are (insert reference to the *Matrix* here).

Before you go out and start holding up banks, randomly tripping people, or kicking small dogs and claiming that it is okay because Krishna said so, it would probably be good to put the idea of actionless action in context. In the Hindu tradition your dharma (duty) is related to both your varna (social class/caste), and ashrama (stages of life). Without getting too far into abstract Hindu theology, which can get more confusing than trying to solve a rubik's cube while blindfolded, it is enough to recognize that in contrast to the American model where we believe we can and should do what we want whenever we want, this system of thought values action in relation to who you are, where you are, and when you are. When we act in this way it is as though we are not acting at all, for it is a reflection of the divine nature of the world. To carry this one step further, just to make sure that you are completely confused, when we act in line with our dharma, varna, and ashrama, we can act without attachment or desire, or in the words of Krishna, "When he renounces all desires and acts without craving, possessiveness, or individuality, he finds peace."[4] This is all to say that acting in accordance with your own particular position in life not only leads to a better life in this world but also to the eternal reward of peace and release from suffering, which sounds like a pretty good deal to me.

Hopefully, you are beginning to get a sense of two major themes in the Hindu tradition: universality, and the importance of social location (unless of course you chose to not read the previous paragraph and have been busy running about on a Krishna-inspired bender). There is one other aspect of the Hindu tradition that we should consider before moving on to other influences on Indian culture, and it is one that all of you anti-American global-citizen types who engage in cultural collage and have taken a yoga class have encountered without even realizing it at the beginning or end of every class when the instructor says the word namaste. Namaste is one of the traditional words used to greet people in India and can roughly be translated as "I see the soul in you."

As charming as this sounds on its own (and to be sure it is a vast leap above our normal, "Hey, what's up) it actually reflects an important aspect of the Hindu tradition: that we are all aspects of the divine being. While there are very, very many schools of thought within Hinduism all of which are very, very good, most recognize that there is a direct and inexorable connection between the personal self (atman) and the ultimate self (Brahman). Again, we are going to try to circumvent prolonged theological discussion for the sake of brevity and to avoid an academic-induced coma, but the important point to remember is that there is a divine aspect to all human beings (yes, even the ones you do not like). This may seem a curious idea to those of us raised in the land of Christ and Cracker Barrel, in which god is wholly other and we are each responsible for our own salvation, but it is an important aspect of Indian religion and culture.

Thus far, we have a picture of a culture in which everyone has a particular duty in relation to both their social location as well as their stage in life, and in which there is the recognition of the divine in each person. This is all well and good for India, but for us Americans who love equality, equal opportunity, choice, and possibility (at least for ourselves and those like us), something here seems unfair. If we are all divine, then why would it be that some of us are born workers and others rulers without the possibility of changing our social position. This is an injustice! It is Unfair! Or perhaps it is just completely misunderstood by those of us who accept linear time. The old adage, that "you only live once," illuminates our drive to achieve as much as we can in this life, attain to the highest possible status, and acquire the largest amount of stuff. This idea is completely foreign to the Indian psyche in which time and human life go through infinite cycles.

The idea that the soul is continually reborn (samsara), and that the world passes through multiple ages (yugas) before being destroyed and reborn all over again, structures the Hindu and to a large degree Indian sense of time (the Indian time zone, IST, is fondly referred to as "Indian Stretch Time"). We Americans are a hurried and stressed people, which makes sense in terms of the belief that we only have one lifetime in which to get everything accomplished (that, combined with an odd quirk in Protestant theology that makes us feel as though we arrive at salvation through getting the nicest stuff—but I will have to save that for another book). Indians, however, with their belief in cyclical time (and massive population in a very small area) take Einstein's route and recognize that time is merely relative.

The problem of having a particular social and temporal position in which you are expected to perform your duty is somewhat mitigated by the Hindu concept of time. You may be a worker (sudra) in this life, but in the next you may be reborn as a ruler (kshatriya), albeit with the current state of politics I am not sure why this would necessarily be a boon since most of the US congress gets slightly less regard than used-car salesmen. This is not to say that there is perfect social harmony in India, for to be sure there is considerable political discontent among the lower castes, particularly the dalit (once known as the untouchables), who feel a tremendous sense of historical marginalization. But even here, the arguments tend to occur within a theological frame with regard to the meaning and interpretation of certain ideas and scriptures. Unlike in America where the debate tends to be between ardent believers and nonbelievers (who curiously end up sounding very similar in their pedantic absolutism), the debate in India is about the meaning and interpretation of the theological ideas of dharma, varna, karma, Vedanta and anything else ending in an—"a." Swami Vivekananda, a much-revered figure in contemporary Hindu thought once said of India that its " . . . life-centre is religion and religion alone. Let others talk of politics, of glory of acquisition of immense wealth poured in by trade, of the power and spread of commercialism, of the glorious fountain of physical liberty; but these the Hindu mind does not understand and does not want to understand."[5] I suppose we all have our purpose.

Like all cultures that have existed over long periods of human history, Indian culture has countless influences, has shifted, developed, and changed forms, and is in no way monolithic. That said, in line with what was put forward in Chapter 2, we can still discern a range of family resemblances that are distinctly Indian (where else are you going to find a McDonald's that sells Aloo Tikki and mutton burgers to appease the large numbers of vegetarians and those who hold the cow to be sacred). The sense of duty in life, the importance of social location, the divinity of the person, and cyclical nature of time are significant elements of this range of family resemblances that manifest themselves in more ways in Indian culture than the Goddess Kali has arms. As strong as an influence as religion may be on India, it is also a modern secular democratic state that is rapidly modernizing, undergoing an economic boom, and poised to become one of the major players in the contemporary geopolitical world. This is to say that while you find countless wandering ascetics, temples, pictures of deities, religious festivals, cows wandering around city streets, and Westerners wandering around in yoga pants, you also find modern skyscrapers, luxury hotels, five-star restaurants, and stylishly dressed Indians staring with a sort of bemused curiosity at the Westerners in yoga pants. To better understand this difficult and yet often amusing dichotomy we need to take a quick look at modern-day India.

A Moment with the Mahatma

Before we reach the modern day, however, we need to first make a quick stop at the beginning of this century to have to consider a man whose influence has been felt the world over, whose figure is memorialized in countless statues throughout India, and whose face is emblazoned upon all Indian currency (as ironic and yet as wonderfully Indian as that might be), the great soul (the translation of mahatma) himself, Gandhi. Gandhi's influence and legacy hover over India like smog over Los Angeles, always present and yet not always directly seen (but in a positive sense of course). From the political dynasty he began that passed through Nehru into today's Congress party, to his treatment of the untouchables who would become the dalit (children of god), the lasting effect of this quiet and yet powerful man cannot be underestimated.

Gandhi's vision for India and the modern, rapidly advancing economic, political, and military power that it has become are almost as distinct as Unitarians and Fundamentalist Christians, and yet like these groups, they share a common thread. In Gandhi's view, the political state of India should be based upon its spiritual inheritances and emphasize the ideas of simplicity, community, cooperation, peace, and an unswerving faith in god. While these ideas may seem utopian and less likely to be realized than finding an Israeli and a Palestinian having a leisurely picnic in the park, Gandhi held until the end of his life that a nation-state founded upon anything less is bound for violence and destruction, a point all too obvious in modern politics. While it is clear that Gandhi's hopes for India have not been fully realized (since I am fairly sure that he never suggested that nuclear weapons are a tool for peace and harmony, nor that call centers in Bangalore were part of a village-based economy, unless you take the idea of the global village a bit too literally), his symbolic influence still remains present in both Indian politics, as well as in the nation's self-identity.

Gandhi was assassinated in 1948 by a Hindu nationalist who was upset over his stance toward Pakistan. In an ironic twist that perhaps sums up the whole of Indian culture, the assassin apologized before he shot Gandhi, while the last words out of the mahatma's mouth were "Hey Ram"—one of the names of god in Hinduism. To understand this curious interchange is to gain better insight into India than you could get by taking a trip down the Ganges (and you are far less likely to get dysentery). By apologizing, Gandhi's assassin was showing him a degree of reverence and respect, and recognizing the power of duty and responsibility. Gandhi in turn was embodying the deep spiritual essence of Indian culture, since it is believed in some parts of the Hindu tradition that your last words are the place to which your soul will attain (I could insert countless jokes here, but it is almost too easy . . .). The sense of cyclical time, duty—even to the point of murder, and spirit, are so built into the Indian worldview that even at the moment of death they are present. I am not sure what this would look like in America, but I think we could exchange an apology for an insult and the name of god for a last-second Twitter or Facebook update ("just been shot—sux, :(").

Thank You for Calling Bangalore, Err . . . I Mean AOL

Now that we have a sense of the father of the Indian state, we can better understand how contemporary India, like many children (not me of course, I was always a dutiful son), has broken away from the hopes and dreams of its parent and set off to find its own course. India at the beginning of the twenty-first century is a vastly different place than it was at the time of the passing of the "great soul." Just recently I saw photographs from the Indian Republic Day parade in which traditionally dressed soldiers rode in on camels in front of a float carrying one of India's newest ballistic missiles. While the camels seemed relatively undisturbed by the advanced weaponry, a human observer from our great land, in which the last time we saw weapons and animals together was in a cowboy movie, might find the transposition of images a bit curious. These seemingly contradictory images bespeak the condition of modern India, standing perched between the advances of modernity and pull of tradition.

To travel through contemporary India is to encounter multiple worlds, multiple realities, and multiple ways to almost die in a car accident—my personal favorite being vehicular bovanicide since cows tend to wander freely across the highways. In one sense, contemporary India is a thoroughly modern, secular democracy. It has a parliamentary system of government and constitution similar to many European countries, enough political parties to almost represent each of the 10,000 gods, and the upper and lower houses of parliament have members from all of the major religious groups. That said, the second largest political party, the Bharatiya Janata Party, is founded upon a Hindu nationalist platform that desires to strengthen and protect India's Hindu roots and culture. Perhaps we should put the Hindu nationalists in touch with the people who want to assert the Christian nature of the United States, albeit I suspect they would somehow not get along due to the whole going-to-hell concept for not accepting the Christ thing.

Directly tied into India's contemporary political landscape are the issues of religion and terrorism. India has long been in conflict with Pakistan over a range of issues, including the disputed borders of Kashmir, and being that these are both nuclear powers these disagreements have global significance. With the growth of transnational terrorist organizations and other shadow groups that are only indirectly linked to official governing bodies, the situation becomes even more confusing than an episode of *Lost*. The terrorist attacks in Mumbai in 2008 revealed the connections between Pakistan's intelligence service, international organizations, and radical Islamic groups within India's own borders. This intricate web of connections makes India's complex political landscape even more confusing as it tries to figure our a way to remain a secular democracy that can protect the rights of the Muslim minority while appeasing the demands of more right-wing nationalist groups. Just in case this is not confusing enough, add to this a growing alliance with the United States, while trying to maintain relationships with old

Soviet-era trading partners and you arrive at a picture so bizarre that even Dali would scratch his head in confusion. Much like India's government, its economy is also in many ways thoroughly modern and yet particularly Indian. Whereas China has moved toward a strong industrial-based economy, India has jumped that step and moved directly to a knowledge-based economy. To think of this in another way, China makes everything that we buy and India provides customer service for it. I have had many fascinating conversations with customer-service representatives in Bangalore, who I am able to awe with my knowledge of their city (and yes I am that bored that I have conversations with phone operators). The Indian economic boom can be seen in the growing middle class, who are more likely to be wearing designer clothes and going out to clubs than donning a sari and performing a temple ritual. While there is economic growth, at least 25 percent of the population still lives in poverty, and nearly 70 percent still live in rural environments. Add to this a level of bureaucracy so complete that trying to get anything done is like trying to convince Brazilian women to give up plastic surgery, and you arrive at a picture of a country in which economic growth and modernization are tempered by broad social and cultural factors.

An event in the state of West Bengal in India offers a telling example of complexity, ambiguity, and at times outright irony of the contemporary Indian economy. Under the leadership of Ratan Tata, the chairman of the Tata Group (An Indian company that seems to make everything from coffee to industrial chemicals—hopefully not at the same factory), Tata Motors developed the worlds smallest car, the aptly named Nano. The idea behind this project is that with the rising wealth of the middle class in India, more people will be able to afford to buy cars and the Nano would be the perfect entry-level vehicle. The car, which everyone except for environmental activists thought was a good idea because it would add to India's already overly polluted air, was not the problem; the problem arose when they tried to find a place to build the factory. An agreement was reached with the chief minister of the state to acquire approximately 1,000 acres of land on which to build a factory, but the farmers assisted by the Communist party, which has a fairly strong presence in West Bengal (maybe Lenin and Mao were right about the revolution but just got the location wrong), staged protests and caused the entire project to be scrapped. So in the end, a twenty-first-century car meant to respond to the needs of a booming modern Indian economy had to be put on hold to appease angry peasants and Communists—it is as though the French, Russian, and Industrial revolutions all decided to occur at the same place at the same time—Vive Le Revolution!

Beyond politics and economics, contemporary India, like all living cultures, continues to undergo transformations in cultural standards, mores, and practices. On one hand, the caste system still has a powerful place in Indian society, particularly with regard to marriage, and, on the other, you see an increasing number of younger Indians insisting on finding love matches and not accepting what their parents choose for them (considering how high the divorce rate is in this country where we all get to choose who we love, people may want to rethink letting their parents decide). The idea of caste has been challenged in another way, where young people are presented with opportunities for work in fields in which their parents could not have imagined, and through education and training may be able to move outside ancient boundaries. That said, inequalities in wealth and access to education still strongly impede the lower castes from gaining access to this increased wealth and upward mobility, but we wouldn't know anything about that in the land of freedom and equality.

Along with shifts in patterns of relationships and social status come changes in social mores that at times coexist more uncomfortably with tradition than if Rush Limbaugh had to share an apartment with a gay, illegal immigrant. A curious example of this tension between tradition and change occurred as a result of a few women frequenting a bar in the Western coastal city of Mangalore. It is becoming more common practice for single women to go out to pubs together, but some more conservative men find this to go against their moral standard. These particular women in Mangalore were harassed and assaulted for going to the pub. Their response, which not even I could make up, was to start a campaign including a facebook page under the title, "The Consortium of pub-going, loose, and forward women," which encourage people to send pink underwear to the group responsible for the attack on Valentine's day. Perhaps that is what we need in this country, more protests involving underwear: camo underwear if you oppose war, green underwear if you are unhappy about the economy, or even underwear made in Mexico if you are a supporter of immigration reform.

As was mentioned in the chapter on culture, shifts in politics, economics, social structure, and morality are the normal course of any living culture or civilization and not something particular to the modern age. Yes, the form may change, but the idea remains the same. It is sort of like playdough. Let's say you get out the good old fun factory, and press the playdough through the star-shaped press. It will come out looking like a star (if it doesn't get jammed or break as was the habit of my fun factory—which made the name somewhat ironic since it wasn't much fun), and yet no one, not even a child, would suggest that it is no longer playdough. This constancy of change may be problematic for certain countries or cultures who become more like dried-out play-dough, because of their inability or unwillingness to accept change. The Christian right in America or fundamentalists in the Muslim world come to mind here. Indian culture with its basis in Hindu universalism and its nonlinear conception of time is the exact opposite. Unlike the desiccated, age-old, crumbly, Christian-right playdough (maybe Jesus dough, since he did say at the last supper that this bread is my body), India would be like the stuff right out of the brand-new container. This is to say that while you do find a Hindu nationalist movement in India, you do not find powerful foes of change and development or the same kind of rampant rejection of modernity and technology that you do in many other countries.

In a sense, we could say that modern India is very much like India has always been, a responsive, adaptable, and universalist place that has a far greater tendency to incorporate new or external influences than to reject or fight against them. All you need to do is look at the number of mustaches on Indian men, or the number of people walking around with umbrellas to see the mark of British influence (admittedly the umbrella is handy to block the sun on those 400-degree days). Or go visit the Taj Mahal, Fatehpur Sikri, Humayun's tomb, or the countless other grand edifices of Shah Jahan to see the influence of Muslim archi-tecture, as well as the enormous egos of the conquering Moguls. In this light, the messy, complicated, loud, vibrant, dynamic, nature of India is not something new but rather something inherent in the place itself.

The pace of change and the amount of things that must be accommodated or adapted to has increased, but the capacity for change, development, and innovation has not. It is as though there are more and more people playing with the playdough, but it is still playdough (don't worry I am done with this metaphor, I will now switch to Silly Putty). Now that I have given you the "very, very best of" tour of India from past to present (I guess I am still stuck in that whole linear time-frame thing), let's try to put it all together into some kind of cohesive picture, or at least one that does not look as messy as, well, India. Looking to the Hindu roots of Modern India, we find a culture that places a strong value upon duty, social location, the unity of all beings, and has a conception of time that is quite distinct from our own. Through Gandhi, who was drawing upon the Hindu faith, we arrive at the emphasis on social welfare, simplicity, and peace that has been somewhat lost but not forgotten since his passing. And through a look at modern India we find a rapidly changing country that has a burgeoning economy and massive poverty, the latest technology and farmers without electricity, and hip restaurants but also monkeys on the street that will come steal your food. I can just imagine the police report that would go along with that: "Yeah, headquarters, we have another 413 over here—a monkey-related theft. The suspect is about a foot-and-a-half tall and is, well, kind of furry like a monkey. Last seen on Gandhi Road, carrying a bag full of bananas and a chapatti."

As should be abundantly, and perhaps amusingly, clear by now, the Indian life world is very much distinct from our own. To say this is to not simply refer to the external trappings (saris vs. dresses, dhotis vs. jeans, chapattis vs. wonder bread, Siva vs. Jesus—Siva clearly wins, he has a trident), but more importantly, to consciousness and a way of being in the world. The Indian orientation is founded upon a distinct set of cultural values, metaphors, and assumptions, which, much like the case with China, do not simply make them encounter the world differently from us, but actually make them encounter a different world—a point that will be addressed in the final chapter. You can wrap yourself in beads, listen to chanting 24 hours a day, and drink nothing but chai (tea with cream) (I do miss a good chai on a hot day—just thinking about it makes me want to plan my next trip), but these things are only the manifestations of a culture and consciousness. India is a complex and dynamic culture, in which the complexity and adaptability are parts of the culture itself. It is for this reason that it is so fascinating, but also so difficult to study and discuss. Perhaps I should just draw pictures, but since my artistic skills seem to have peaked around grade 3, how about we just go watch some more TV.

Notes

1 Sharma, Arvind. *Our Religions: The Seven World Religions Introduced by Preeminent Scholars from Each Tradition.* HarperOne, 1994, p. 4.

2 Ibid, p. 5.

3 Miller, Barbara Stoler. *The Bhagavad-Gita : Krishna's Counsel in Time of War.* Bantam Classics, 1986. see chapter 2.

4 Ibid.

5 http://www.boloji.com/hinduism/00601.htm

Suggestions for Further Reading

Eck, Diana L. *Darshan: Seeing the Divine Image in India.* 3rd ed. Columbia University Press, 1998.

Embree, Ainslee. *Sources of Indian Tradition, Vol. 1: From the Beginning to 1800.* 2nd ed. Columbia University Press, 1988.

Guha, Ramachandra. *India After Gandhi: The History of the World's Largest Democracy.* Reprint. Harper Perennial, 2008.

Kamdar, Mira. *Planet India: The Turbulent Rise of the Largest Democracy and the Future of Our World.* Scribner, 2008.

Luce, Edward. *In Spite of the Gods: The Rise of Modern India.* Anchor, 2008.

Meredith, Robyn. *The Elephant and the Dragon: The Rise of India and China and What It Means for All of Us.* W.W. Norton & Co., 2008.

Miller, Barbara Stoler. *The Bhagavad-Gita : Krishna's Counsel in Time of War.* Bantam Classics, 1986.

Rajagopalachari, C. *Ramayana.* Bharatiya Vidya Bhavan/Mumbai/India, 2007.

Sharma, Arvind. *A Guide to Hindu Spirituality.* World Wisdom, 2006.

—. *Our Religions: The Seven World Religions Introduced by Preeminent Scholars from Each Tradition.* HarperOne, 1994.

Stein, Burton. *A History of India.* Wiley-Blackwell, 1998.

6

Watching TV in India

Hey You Can Watch TV on TV Here

Here again, as in Chapter 4, we are going to leave out the exercise. I would offer some philosophical justification about how this, like chapter 4, is an extended exercise in cultural analysis, where we will spend considerable time viewing specific examples of American programming through an Indian lens so a separate preparation is not necessary. Or perhaps that since the ground work was laid in the previous chapter, it would be better to jump right into our discussion about watching TV in India. Or maybe even that separating theoria and praxis ultimately undermines our full capacity for understanding our subject. But I think I will stick with something a bit more pragmatic like absolute exhaustion from the jet lag.

My first trip to India went nothing like my first trip to China. Well, maybe not nothing. There were seedy hotels (someone needs a bigger research budget), copious amounts of sweating as a result of ungodly (or I suppose in this case un-Vishnuly) temperatures, and so much pollution that I actually took up smoking to give my lungs a break from the air. Despite these similarities, my experiences in these places, like those of anyone who has traveled to both places, could not have been more different. For the moment, at least, the primary point of difference that we need to be concerned about is that I was able to watch TV, on TV. Yes, I was able to sit right down on my bed that felt as though it was made out of gravel and hay, covered in a velour blanket that seemed to have been left over from a 70s porn movie, reach for the remote control being held together by rubber bands, push the power button, and after the 17th blackout of the day ended, watch the TV flicker on to satellite cable, where I saw the familiar glowing warmth of American TV programming.

My trip to India did not require me to buy bootleg DVDs, find creative ways to circumvent ever-growing governmental control over the Internet, or otherwise overcome strict limits on the freedom of media and information. As the world's largest democracy with increasing liberalization in law and economics, the Indian population has broad access to media sources, including television programming from around the world. In fact, there are currently over 300 different satellite channels available to the Indian market (of course, the second I write this, this figure will be completely wrong, and by the time the book get to the market it will be even more incorrect, but that just shows how rapidly these markets are changing. And anyway, you get the idea). Add to this the rapid growth of the cable television market that has gone from around 22 million households in 1999, to close to 75 million today (another figure that will likely be outdated by the time this book comes to print) and you have about as many people tuning in to cable TV in India as you have in the United States.[1] But much like India itself, the meaning of these figures is complex, changing, and at times outright confusing.

As open as the cable market in India is today, it has not actually been that way for very long. Until the early 1990s television in India, while not completely state owned, was closely regulated by the national government and developed through a single broadcaster called Doordarshan (which shockingly translates into tele-vision). While this seems as though the Indian government were taking a page out of Mao's little red handbook on media control, they were in fact pursuing very different ends. Unlike China that was specifically attempting to control access to information, Doordarshan's goal was to act as a medium for nation-building and national integration.[2] From our perspective this may seem a bit curious. Admittedly, if you were to turn on the TV and all you could watch were shows about American history and culture, you would probably think that the Republicans had finally succeeded it taking over the country and have begun instituting their Orwellian plan of total mind control. If, however, you remember from the last chapter that India is actually a far more diverse country than we tend to realize, with at least 17 different languages, distinct cultural traditions, and religious population, and that prior to twentieth century there was no sense of a cohesive Indian state, the use of television as a medium for national integration begins to make more sense (and seem somewhat less terrifying). Whether or not Doordarshan had much of an impact in its early years is a matter for debate, with some people seeing it as doing little more than enforcing a Hindu and Hindi vision on India against all of the other linguistic and ethnic groups. It would almost be as if the official televised vision of America sent out to all American homes was based upon the New York area (which, since Neo-Nazis and Skinheads are usually spot on, and they claim that the Jews control the media, may well be the case).

You Will Obey Rupert Murdoch

The foreign television invasion began in India in 1991 with the worlds favorite tabloid, I mean news source, CNN.[3] Soon after this, a broad range of satellite networks began beaming into and operating out of India, with Rupert Murdoch's Star Networks taking the lead among foreign companies (not that we should be surprised since he owns half the media companies in the world at this point—I hope he doesn't own my publisher). What is particularly interesting, however, is that rather than Indian audiences clamoring for foreign television shows, they instead were more interested in Indian programming, leading Murdoch to have to make adjustments to his market strategy.[4] To this day, Indian programming remains more popular than foreign shows, American included, something quite different from the rampant consumption of American TV programming in China (where, ironically, you can't get it on TV—we always want what we cannot have). If anything, regional cable stations that broadcast in the local languages (Tamil in particular, since Tamils are fiercely proud of their distinct language and culture, something I was informed of during a speech/tirade/soliloquy by a cashier at a restaurant somewhere in the western mountains of Tamil Nadu) have been increasing in popularity in India in recent years.

Rupert Murdoch was not alone in having to "Indianize" his media empire; the majority of foreign companies that have tried to find a space in the Indian television market have had to adapt their programming for the Indian context.[5] This is a fascinating point in terms of the discussion about globalization in Chapter 1. Not to disappoint all those antiglobalization protesters beating on drums and carrying signs with oh-so-clever slogans at the latest meeting of the G8/G12/UN/World Bank/IMF/ NRA/QVC/HSN, but this is not a one-way system of domination and power. The liberalization of the Indian television market does reveal that we cannot simply impose one culture on another and assume that it will be received and accepted. Rather, the interaction between cultures is far more subtle, complex, and textured and does not simply operate through imposition of power alone as suggested by Derrida and his fellow angsty postmodern friends (I think all of those French intellectuals need to cheer up by spending some time at the happiest place in Europe: Euro Disney). The important point here is that, as we have been discussing through out the book, we bring our cultural metaphors with us to everything we encounter, and if the programming we are watching does not fit, it will not have an audience.

There is one more point worth addressing about the Indian television market before we move on to analyzing specific programs, and that is that it is Indian. This is to say that while there may be millions of homes with cable television access, there are still significant portions of the population living in rural areas with no electricity. There are hundreds of millions of dollars being invested into information and infrastructure upgrades in India, including extensive fiber-optic networks, but the amount of red tape and bureaucracy that goes into getting this started makes us look like we actually have a functional government. And while liberalization of the market has led to increased programming it has not been regulated, meaning that anyone and their mother (literally) can run some wires and claim to have a cable company. The current estimate is that there is somewhere between 30,000 to 60,000 providers.[6] Do not get me wrong; living in New York City and having to sell pints of blood just to cover my TimeWarner cable bill does make me desire some open competition in the market (or at least to learn how to steal cable), but there may be a middle ground between 1 company and 10,000. Beyond this immense confusion in trying to set up your account ("Yes, I would like to set up an account with Singh Cable." "Which one sir, there are

2,734 Singh cable listed in Delhi"), it also leads to an inconsistency in access to programming as well as significant problems with reliability. This is all to say that while cable television and access to American programming is widely available in India, the television market itself continues to undergo considerable growth and change. We are now going to change our focus and move from structure to content, from surface to depth, from existence to essence, from the hard-candy shell to the inner tootsie-roll goodness. As we did with the chapter on China, we have to begin with the realization that there is also no one single type of Indian television viewer. Lal Krishna Advani, Patel Sudhakar Reddy, and Mayawati would all clearly have significantly different understandings of *The Price is Right* (I know you have no idea who these people are, but the one person reading this book who knows about Indian politics is laughing hysterically right now—trust me). That said, as was the case with China, there are webs of meaning and interconnection and groups of family resemblances that allow us to speak of an Indian perspective. In fact, this idea was well expressed by everyone's favorite politician in a pants suit, Secretary of State Hillary Rodham Clinton. On a trip to India while discussing cultural understanding with a group of students said,

People watching a Bollywood movie in some other part of Asia think everybody in India is beautiful, and they have dramatic lives and happy endings. And if you were to watch American TV and our movies, you think we don't wear clothes and we spend a lot of time fighting each other.[7]

As Clinton so nicely points out, in the face of all the difference and diversity, we Americans do spend a lot of time naked and fighting.

Since you can actually watch TV on TV in India and do not have to find creative ways to circumvent Internet control or buy bootleg DVD of questionable quality on the street, the choice of programming to discuss is limited. Yes, I did mean to write limited. The curious upside to having the majority of American programming viewed as a corrupting influence in China is that there are no corporate media conglomerates deciding what Chinese people want to watch, instead the people themselves have to seek out what they find interesting. In India on the other hand you have big brother (a.k.a Rupert Murdoch) and the world state (a.k.a Newscorp) deciding in advance what is available and popular (convenient if you are 16-year-old girl who wants to fit in, but not if you actually value choice). This means that the primary channel that carries American programming in India, Star World, has a curious menagerie of programs drawn from all of the US broadcast networks. So any given day you may have the chance to watch *Ellen*, *Are You Smarter than a Fifth Grader*, 14 episodes of *Friends* (I am starting to think that watching *Friends* may be the key to world peace), *Grey's Anatomy*, and *Everybody Loves Raymond*. I believe that my initial reaction to watching Star World on my first trip to India was something akin to "Who the hell is picking this stuff." After my surprise at *My Name is Earl* being shown outside the country, since I did not even realize that it was shown in the country, I began to realize that even Newscorp had to respond to its audience to some degree and that each of these programs must in some way be open to an encounter with Indian cultural metaphors.

More Mind-Numbing Goodness

While India does have its own set of companies to akin to the Nielson ratings that measures television shows' popularity, their quality, reach, and effectiveness is more questionable than Sarah Palin's grasp of sentence structure. Because of this, unlike for the chapter on China where we picked programs on the basis of their popularity, in this case we will have to pick them on the basis of their availability to the Indian market. The programs that we will consider also share a couple of other things in common. While we may not be able to measure their relative popularity in India, they all are or have been popular in the American market. Also, like the shows chosen for Chapter 4, each of these programs opens a horizon for cultural analysis and comparison. That said, another similarity with Chapter 4 is that beyond these points, the shows have nothing in common. The themes, genre, structure, format, images, and American target audiences are all distinct, making it once again an interesting point that all three of these shows can cross-cultural boundaries. Now that we have all that out of the way grab your favorite chaat, bhel puri, or some papadams and get ready to watch *The Simpsons*, *Heroes*, and *The OC*.

The Simpsons

In some ways it is difficult to believe that *The Simpsons* has been around for 20 years, has aired over 400 episodes, and remains popular both here in its country of birth and around the world. While *The Simpsons* has long since passed as a phenomenon, although I do fondly remember being 10 years old and buying a t-shirt emblazoned with the words cowabunga dude (my fashion sense has somewhat improved), it remains a significant cultural force in the United States. In fact, it has even affected the way we speak with Homer's famous explicative, D'oh, actually finding a place in the *Oxford English Dictionary*. It has also been a powerful cultural force around the world, as it has been broadcast into countless nations and translated into numerous languages—sometimes with curious consequences. In one instance in Quebec, where there is a surprising degree of hatred directed toward the Jews to the point of having one of the metro stations named for a known anti-Semitic priest, a line about boycotting Krusty the Klown's products is translated into "Let's have a holocaust."[8] While this is an extreme example (I hope), it does illustrate our point about the multivocal nature of programming once it leaves its country of origin even if that voice is one of hatred or racism.

I am not going to try to unpack the cultural, philosophical, socio-logical, anthropological, psychological, soteriological (look it up, it's a good scrabble word), or eschatological meaning of *The Simpsons* in America. There are already enough books on the subject to fill all the bookshelves at the perfectly designed sample rooms at Ikea (which are kind of creepy and yet always make me want to redecorate). Instead of some grand theory on the cosmology of *The Simpsons* I am going to offer the obvious—it is a clever satire. It is a show that has done a very good job of playing off the major political, socioeconomic, and cultural issues that we have struggled with as a country over the past 20 years. To the extent that this is the case, the more you understand about these issues, the funnier and more engaging the show is (just call me "Captain Obvious"). It is not that the show cannot be enjoyed without keeping up with the current events and cultural trends, but to an American audience no small part of the appeal of the program is laughing at ourselves and our own cultural and political debacles—and we do have plenty to laugh at. Cartoons in general are an interesting genre for this reason; they provide a space to say and do things that you could never get away with human actors (and not just because they disobey the laws of physics). Whether it is Tony the Italian gangster, Willie the grounds-keeper Scotsman, or Apu the Quickee Mart clerk, *The Simpsons* is able to ply in cultural stereotypes and in a way that would get most programs pulled off the air.

The fact that *The Simpsons* is a clever satire that provides us with the capacity to laugh at ourselves does nothing, however, to help explain its appeal or meaning in India. In many ways, this entire layer of the show becomes irrelevant or at least inaccessible once it crosses cultural boundaries, since all of the cultural background and metaphors that would make it funny are no longer present. It would sort of be like bring-ing a bathing suit to Antarctica; sure you have it but its not going to do you a whole lot of good. So if the satire is the bathing suit, then there has to be something else in *The Simpsons* luggage that is useful. To overex-tend this already pained metaphor, the long johns, in the luggage would be the characters. *The Simpson* family and their associated friends, neighbors, colleagues, and classmates, while originally placed in the surroundings of Springfield, anywhere America, are multivocal images that allow for multiple encounters and interpretations that easily cross cultural boundaries. We will look at two examples.

Homer Simpson, from the American perspective, does not appear to be a paradigm of virtue. He is character who commits a cardinal sin against the American way of life in that he has no particular aspirations, does not strive to attain the nicest stuff, and just generally floats by through life (apparently he didn't get the BBM about working yourself to death). There is a particularly telling interaction between him and the character Frank Grimes from season 8. When Grimes, who is a hard-working, pull-yourself-up-by-the-bootstraps kind of guy, sees Homers house, family, and all that he has accomplished in life, he is shocked and appalled that a man with such a passive attitude could do so well. In this, he is expressing the general American belief that we must struggle, face adversity, and make our own way in the world, as though we were all somehow Davy Crocket or Horatio Alger. In this light Homer seems passive and apathetic, that is, of course unless he is enlightened. If you think back to the last chapter, one of the central aspects in Hinduism is the idea of dharma (responsibility/duty) and that we each must fulfill this according to our position in life. The more aligned we are with our dharma, the less struggle and strife we will face in our lives. When you receive the world as it is and do not work against it for your own sake, your own life as well as everyone's around you will be better. Without insulting any of my Hindu friends, or the other 800 million around the world, perhaps Homer is not lazy at all but simply does not accept the Christian work ethic (he does hate going to church) and instead embraces the Hindu worldview (he does like dressing up as Ganesha).

If Homer represents everything that is wrong with the American worker, at least to us, then Bart represents everything that is wrong with American youth. Bart is impetuous, disrespectful, cunning, self-interested, and for the most part seems to lack the capacity for empathy or compassion. This is not to say that he is all bad, just that from our perspective he is the embodiment of every CNN, MSNBC, Fox News, headline about how the youth of today has gone astray (little matter, of course, that every generation thinks this of the next, but perhaps this time we are right). The idea of the not simply corrupt but, in a sense, despairing nature of American youth is so common to our culture that we do not even question it when we see it—Bart just makes sense. Walk the streets of India on the other hand, and you find something different. The rapid pace of change and economic growth that we discussed in the last chapter leads to a situation in which often times Indians, particularly the younger generation, have to, let's put it politely and say, "get creative," to find sources of income. Interestingly, the majority of wealth in India's economy is still driven by what are referred to as cottage industries, things that are outside the corporate marketplace. This type of economy can range from Gandhi's idea of home-spun cotton to things that would make the mahatma rethink his stance of nonviolence, like touts at the airport tricking tourists into going to a hotel where they get a kickback, by telling people that the hotel they had booked had burned down/blown up/been reincarnated as a McDonalds. In this type of economy being smart (cunning), industrious (self-interested), and calculating (lack of empathy) can be viewed as virtues rather than vices. So whereas Bart may represent the downfall of the younger generation to us, he could be seen as the embodiment of the spirit of the younger generation in India.

What both Homer and Bart demonstrate is that Americans tend to have a somewhat negative self-evaluation (perhaps justifiably, since we are home to Hannah Montana and High School Musical) and that we enjoy laughing at our own issues, concerns, and mediocrity. What they say about us to ourselves, however, is very different from what they say to an Indian audience. If you replace the Protestant work ethic and a well-regulated economy (relatively speaking) with dharma and a developing economy, you arrive at a view of Homer, Bart, and the American identity that resonates with both India's past and present. In a sense, Americans become people who are both wiling to accept their social position as well find creative ways to get by, and America becomes the kind of place in which this is possible. This is certainly not what we are like to ourselves, but as we will discuss in the next chapter that is only half the story.

Heroes

The question of who we see ourselves as versus how the rest of the world sees us leads us to our next program, Heroes. For those unfamiliar with the show it is about the multiple attempts at taking over, controlling, destroying, fixing, saving the world by people who have super powers, and how this plays itself out through multiple, complex plot twists and clever cliffhangers. It is actually a rather engaging show if for no other reason than it allows you to ponder one of life's great question: What super power would you want and why (I have always wanted the ability to walk on water, turn water into wine, and be resurrected, but this may stem from my mild messianic complex). This question is not trivial, particularly in so far as how we answer, both as an individual and as a culture, reveals a tremendous amount about us. The fact that a show about people with special powers is popular among a mainstream American audience and not just the *Star Trek* convention–attending, Klingon-speaking, comic-buying, Dungeons and Dragons–playing set who tend to be found in their parent's basement is in itself somewhat interesting. Add to this that it is able to cross cultural boundaries, and you have something worthy of consideration.

From the American perspective, Heroes plays upon one of the most common cultural metaphors/collective neurosis of the day, narcissism.

It has become fairly common over the last couple of decades to suggest that we are a generation of narcissists, a point that most of you reading this right now would agree with—with regards to everyone but yourself of course (you are perfect just the way you are). This idea of narcissism tends to be misunderstood. When everyone's favorite coke-snorting, cigar-smoking, mother-hating psychologist first suggested the idea he did not mean that the narcissist was possessed by inordinate self-love. What Freud was actually suggesting was that the narcissist actually feels empty inside and masks this emptiness through a fragile shell of self-importance and egoism. This is to say that when you see people walking down the street dressed like celebrities with their giant sunglasses, Louis Vuitton purse, $375 designer jeans, designer *dog de jour* (I am going for the Bulldog–Shitzu mix), what they really are expressing, according to this theory at least, is their deep-seated emptiness and the meaninglessness of their lives. We do not have to fully agree with the theory of narcissism to recognize that, much like in Chapter 4 when we discussed *Lost*, we can easily notice a powerful feeling of emptiness, purposelessness, meaninglessness, pointlessness, and a general feeling of ennui (what a great word) hanging over contemporary American culture like a dark cloud. With this somewhat depressive cultural milieu as a background, it is not hard to see how a show that offers both heroism and the idea of being special would be attractive.

The metaphors of despair and emptiness, while big in America, do not really find an audience in India. In fact, recent studies have shown that Indians, particularly Indian youth, are some of the most optimistic people right now in terms of their lives and future prospects (must be nice to actually believe in a positive vision of the future—we wouldn't know anything about that). If *Heroes* is not playing upon American malaise, there must be something else that the Indian viewer is encountering. While few Americans have had the occasion to encounter Indian mythology, it is infinitely fascinating, morally complex, and often involves multilayered and twisting plots in which gods become manifest on Earth and interact, and sometimes even work together with humans. Just in case you had a late night last night, are feeling a bit slow, and are not picking up the parallels, this sounds an awful lot like *Heroes*. While the characters with superpowers in *Heroes* are certainly not gods, they do posses what could be considered godly abilities and are involved in morally confusing situations and are even paired with the average folks without powers. *Heroes* may not be on par with the great Indian Epics like the Ramayana or the Mahabharata (albeit for those who have seen the Indian made-for-TV versions of these, you know that they make public-access TV look like high-quality production), but for those who have been raised with the stories of Rama (the seventh incarnation of Vishnu), Sita (his wife), Hanuman (his monkey-headed god friend— again, I couldn't make this up), Krishna (the eighth incarnation of Vishnu), and the whole Kaurava (bad guys) and Pandava (good guys) clans, it does fit nicely within the genre. In this light, *Heroes* becomes a struggle of good versus evil, right versus wrong, justice versus injustice, and all those other religious and moral struggles, rather than yet another reflection of our cultural boredom and narcissism (I'll take the former please).

Speaking of Indian epics, our friend Krishna from the last chapter offers another interesting insight into *Heroes* from the Indian perspective. As those of you who went on Krishna-related benders will recall, the eighth incarnation of Vishnu's point was that our actions are not our own and we are called upon to perform our dharma without attachment to the outcomes of our actions. Throughout *Heroes*, particularly in the character of *Hiro*, but in others as well, the idea of having to do what needs to be done is quite common. Whether it is Hiro saving the cheerleader, Peter saving the world, Nathan saving Peter, Noah saving Claire, or any of the other countless crises from which people need saving, everyone always seems to be doing what is necessary without regard to their own personal well-being. The "good" characters on the show are always following their dharma and acting without thought of personal gain or loss (how un-American! They must all be communists), whereas the "bad" characters are trying to manipulate the world for their own ends (that's the American spirit). Whereas the idea of doing our duty, serving others, and being heroic has become almost quaint and outdated in American culture, to the point where the old-style heroes that rose up after the Second World War, like Captain America, have actually been killed off and the ones that remain are morally ambivalent antiheroes like Batman or John McClane (not that I don't love *Die Hard*), this is not the case in India. The ideas of duty and responsibility are understood differently in the land of Gandhi than they are in the land of gun violence, and this leads to a distinct encounter of *Heroes* that reflects a more positive vision.

One more point worth addressing about *Heroes* before moving on is time. A number of programs, including *Heroes* and *Lost*, have recently gone the way of Michael J. Fox in the 80s and have taken to using time travel. The idea of time travel is nothing new in itself, but the fact that it is becoming increasingly more prevalent in popular programs is sort of interesting. Throughout *Heroes*, you find multiple examples of people from the past, present, and future interacting, and sometime even multiple incarnations of the same person from different times (I have personally always wanted to go back and make some fashion suggestions to my previous self, but it was the 90s so it wasn't really my fault). From our perspective, the idea of multiple-times coexisting is philosophically, religiously, and scientifically problematic, but represents a general cultural attitude of dissatisfaction and the wish that we could do it all over again (e.g., the midlife crisis—ponytail, red corvette, 21-year-old girl friend and all). Indian audiences have neither our sense of disappointment with our lives (not me of course, I'm fantastic) or our sense of linear time. Indians, as we have already discussed, are generally fairly optimistic and have a sense of time that is cyclical, if not perhaps nonexistent (a point made abundantly clear when standing at a train station waiting for a train, that is 3 hours, to be continually informed that it is on time and "not a problem"). This is all to say that differing conceptions of time lead to very different understandings of the world. Once again it seems that how we see ourselves and how we are seen by others strongly diverges.

The OC

Before we move on to directly discuss the discrepancy between our self-understanding as Americans and how we are viewed by those of other cultures, we will make one last stop in front of the TV. For this stop we are going to have to head over to the west coast, to the land of blonde hair, surfboards, Bodybuilder governors, smog, aspiring stars, gluttony, lust, jealousy (well, pretty much all the seven deadly sins) and people who still use the word "dude." Not just any place in California will do (I have a personal preference for Disneyland), we have to go to the bastion of new money and broken families (they do seem to go together), *The OC*. As much as I enjoyed the soundtrack for the OC, having never truly outgrown my old hardcore music days, I cannot say that I ever fully developed an appreciation for the show. It may well be a generational thing, since when I informed one of my favorite students that I would be writing about *The OC* her reaction was, "Oh my god! I love The OC! It is like one of my favorite shows. You know what else you should write about, *Gilmore Girls*, it is so good." When I informed her that *Gilmore Girls* was not shown in India, she was somewhat disappointed but still "soooo excited" that I was writing about *The OC*. While it only ran for four seasons it developed a dedicated, and apparently excitable, fan base in the United States, and became one of the shows picked up by Star World.

For those unfamiliar with the show it is basically a teenage soap opera, in the same vein as *My So Called Life*, *90210*, and *Gossip Girl*, which revolves around the lives of a group of wealthy families living in, oddly enough, Orange County and what happens when a young man with a troubled past gets thrown into the mix. As you might imagine, the plot lines tend to involve drugs, alcohol, falling in love, breaking-up; drugs, parties, breaking-up, music, breaking-up; alcohol, cheating on people, and, well, breaking-up. While it is always difficult to say why things are popular with teenagers, since when you ask them the response tends to be "I don't know, I just like it," *The OC*, like many of the current lot of teenage dramas tends to embody and express certain aspects of contemporary youth culture. In a sense the show is operating on two levels. There is the surface encounter of "Its just like my life. I totally know what she was feeling when he cheated on her with that girl. He is such a jerk, how could he do that to her" (I have clearly spent too much time around teenagers). And then there are the deeper cultural aspects that are in many ways similar to those we have previously discussed, particularly narcissism and pessimism. To watch *The OC* from an American perspective is not to encounter something happy and light hearted, it is to be a witness to economic excess, psychological suffering, and dysfunctional relationships—sound familiar?

The distance between California and India is millions of miles (it is actually around 8005, but I was being metaphorical). While multi-million-dollar homes, posh rides, and designer clothes are on the rise in

India, it is far more common to find decaying buildings, 4 people on one mechanically unsound motorbike, and the ubiquitous plaid shirt or sari. Similarly while all families have their problems, rampant drug abuse, alcoholism, and infidelity probably come in a bit behind money, safety, and the occasional elephant trampling for most Indians. While the average Indian viewer would have little in common with a citizen of *The OC*, at least on the surface, the images and characters are multivocal enough for the show to resonate with Indian audiences as well. In part the ability for Indians to appreciate this show is the very fact that they do not carry certain cultural metaphors and that they do not encounter the same type of narcissism or cultural pessimism when they watch it. There may be dysfunctional families and troubled relationships, but they are occurring in an environment that even wealthy Indians do not often enjoy. Anyone who goes to the prosperous sections of Delhi or Mumbai will see mansions next to hovels, manicured lawns surrounded by piles of trash, and Mercedes driving down roads with broken-down trucks, autorickshaws, and cows. As we discussed in the previous chapter, India is a rapidly developing economy, but still developing. So in India, where the average person lives on a couple of dollars a day, what attracts viewers to *The OC* may not be so much what they share in common as what they do not.

Beyond the portrayals of a world that most Indians can only imagine in terms of wealth and environment, there is something else that makes *The OC* attractive in India. In a point that would seem strange if it did not somehow make perfect sense, Indian audiences love soap operas. In fact, some of the first American programs that were available to the upper-class Indians who could afford it were shows like *Dallas* and *As the World Turns* (I am more of a *Days of Our Lives* fan—any show that can work in exorcism is okay with me). The reason I say this is that it is almost strange that just as Heroes is able to draw upon the cultural background of great Indian epics, so too are soap Operas like *The OC*. Even though there may not be gods or godly figures in these shows (although I suppose that it could be argued that Mischa Barton is sort of godly in a different kind of way), they are still complex dramas that convey familial struggles, disputes over power, and convey conflicts between good and evil (Ryan and Trey). In a sense, a show like *The OC*, as a soap opera, becomes a screen onto which Indian cultural metaphors

and can be easily projected, a point made even more clear by the preva-
lence of these kinds of programs on Star TV (*Heroes, The OC, Grey's
Anatomy, Desperate Housewives, Lipstick Jungle, Are You Smarter Than a
Fifth Grader*—well, not the last one, but it does air on Star TV). So the
Indian viewer is not really encountering American melodrama as much
as an Indian cultural inheritance.

While television may be widespread in India, and English may be the
lingua franca (in your face France), as was mentioned previously
English-language television remains less popular than programming in
local languages. This in small part is due to the fact that while most
people speak some degree of English, only the wealthier classes are truly
conversant. This point becomes abundantly clear after asking people on
the street for information or directions. Everyone wants to be helpful so
they will answer you, whether they understand or not, and just make
stuff up if they do not. Me: "Is the Taj Mahal this way." Reply: "Yes it is
very beautiful." Me: "Right, but is this how I get there." Reply: "It is very
good." Me: "Uhh . . . uhh . . . uhh . . . right." Reply: [head wobble and
smile]. The more educated that someone is the more likely they are to
speak English fluently; the higher someone's varna/caste, the more likely
they are to be educated. And the greater degree of fluency in English, the
more likely someone is to watch American programming.

If we use some basic logic (and I know we are getting near the end of
the chapter; you may be tired, so I wont ask for too much mental exer-
tion) we arrive at the fact that those of higher social status are more
likely to be viewers of American programming like *The OC* that largely
conveys images of people of upper classes. To carry this one step further,
it is possible to suggest (well, it must be possible since I am doing it—so
that is probably an unnecessary qualifier) that part of what is attractive
about *The OC* to Indian audiences is this very notion of class/caste consciousness. While there has been some change with regard to awareness
of caste, it still plays a major role in Indian society and, as we discussed
in the last chapter, is a significant part of India's cultural background.
Whereas in the United States when we watch *The OC* we do so with
either jealousy and desire, or after the financial crisis, a level of nausea
similar to going on a carnival ride after eating a funnel cake, in India
they see something that is very much built into their social structure.
This lifestyle does not necessarily come off as greedy or selfish, but more
just as part of the way the world is.

In what should be a rather obvious statement at this point, *The OC,* *Heroes,* and *The Simpsons* share nothing in common with one another, except for the fact that they each present a series of images, characters, and situations that are multivocal and open to multiple interpretations. In saying this, we end up exactly where we ended the chapter on China, and where we began this chapter (maybe Nietzsche was right about eternal return). In this case ending where we begin is not a bad thing, since it helps us to recognize that in many ways the program being viewed is far less important than what is brought to the program. Yes, there has to be something to hang our cultural metaphors on, but like we discussed in the first chapter, living cultures are highly adaptable and can fit many phenomenon within their boundaries. So when someone from India is watching *The OC* the fact that they do not know American culture does not matter, since in the end they are watching their own cultural metaphors, values, and ideas into the program. *The OC* in a way becomes *The SM* (Southern Mumbai—a relatively nice section of the city where many wealthy families live).

Even though these shows have nothing in common on the surface, by looking at all three of them, a couple of interesting points come out. First, many of the programs that are popular in our own great land have a tendency to show us as having not such a great land, at least from our own perspective. On the other hand, from the Indian perspective we arrive at something that is more subtle and complex, and in the end paints a very different picture of American culture and the American identity than we encounter when we watch the same programs. Dharma, varna, and economic development replace narcissism, individualism, greed, and pessimism. Before anyone stands up and begins to yell about how they do not see things this way, I just want to once again be clear, that these are not universal perspectives and there are of course degrees of variance; however, for the sake of dialogue and consideration we need at least a base line to work from.

This chapter, much like Chapter 4 has been an attempt to demonstrate how when we begin with distinct cultural paradigms and metaphors we arrive at what are ostensibly different programs. It would be like if someone from Springfield, Kentucky, and someone from Orange County, California, were to both take a road trip to Las Vegas. Each family, let's respectively name them the Cohens and the Simpsons, would drive along completely different roads, see distinct scenery, have unique sets of irritating car games that are meant to pass time but rather make it seem as though you are approaching the speed of light (for those less familiar with the theory of relativity, time is suppose to slow down). When they arrive at Las Vegas, each family will have their own sets of responses (garish and tacky vs sinful—should have gone to Branson), see different sites, stay at different oddly themed hotels (I like the one with the pirate ship), and then return to their respective homes. While we can fairly say that at the end of their adventures the Cohens and the Simpsons each saw the physical place called Las Vegas, what that means to each will be about as similar as Cracker Barrel and the Rainbow Room. In the next chapter we are going to begin working out what this means in terms our self-understanding and how we are viewed by others around the world.

Notes

1. "India Cable TV Origin" http://indiancabletv.net/cabletvhistory.htm.
2. Pashupati, Kartik, Hua Lin Sun, and Stephen D. McDowell. "Guardians of Culture, Development Communicators, or State Capitalists?: A Comparative Analysis of Indian and Chinese Policy Responses to Broadcast, Cable and Satellite Television." *Gazette* 65, no. 3 (June 1, 2003): 259.
3. Sinclair, John, and Mark Harrison. "Globalization, Nation, and Television in Asia: The Cases of India and China." *Television New Media* 5, no. 1 (February 1, 2004): 44.
4. Ibid, p. 45.
5. Thussu, D. K. "Privatizing the Airwaves: The Impact of Globalization on Broadcasting in India." *Media, Culture & Society* 21, no. 1 (1, 1999): 127.
6. "TakingITGlobal—Panorama—Cable TV in India." http://www.tigweb.org/express/panorama/article.html?ContentID=1098.
7. "Clinton Reaches Out to New Generation in India: NPR." http://www.npr.org/templates/story/story.php?storyId=106795154.
8. "The Simpsons Archive: Simpsons, in Theory." http://snpp.com/other/articles/simpsonsintheory.html.

7

This Is America

Exercise #5

Now that you have had a chapter off to rest and relax, it is time to get back to the exercises (you are starting to look a little intellectually paunchy). We will start off slowly, however, so that you do not pull a muscle, or I suppose in this case a synapse, or neuron, or whatever fires off when you use your brain. I am going to ask you to do something that should seem a bit familiar from Chapter 1; I want you to put down the book (you know the drill by now) and write down everything that comes to mind when you hear the word *America*.

(I will hum the national anthem, God Bless America, America the Beautiful, the Battle Hymn of the Republic, and Hit Me Baby One More Time while you work).

The possible range of answers to this question is almost limitless. Perhaps you wrote about purple mountains majesty and shining seas, or urban blight and the rust belt. Maybe you thought about freedom, liberty, democracy, and equality, Superman, Captain America, and the American way, or perhaps about the fact that we have a greater percentage of our population in prison than any other country in the world, disenfranchised voters, a strong correlation between race and poverty, and idolize people like Paris Hilton, and that trumped the Norman Rockwell idea of America. Then again you may have taken a different route completely and focused on the fact that our great nation leads the world in innovations in science, technology, and medicine, and how many of these technological advances came out of money spent on military development and defense spending, which has in turn been used to kill people from other nations not quite as great as us. Regardless of what is on your list, I want you to pay attention to the tone of your list. Are most of the things you have picked positive or negative? The kind of feelings and emotions that are associated with the words you have chosen are probably more telling about your idea of America than the stuff you actually listed.

Next, instead of thinking about the America as a place I want you to think about the people and write down what comes to mind when you hear the word *American*. (Here I think I will hum a selection from Bruce Springsteen, Neil Diamond, Tom Petty, Public Enemy, and Lee Greenwood—for balance).

There will probably be some overlap with your previous list, but you should also find some unique points. Perhaps your lists included such things as brave, strong, creative, adventurous, independent, free, hard working, and god fearing. Perhaps. But if you are reading this book it means that you have an interest in such things as identity, culture, and communication, which also means that you probably have a higher-than-average degree of education or at least intellectual curiosity, which in turn means your list probably includes words like, fat, lazy, stupid, arrogant, greedy, fat, corrupt, self-interested, fat, and moralizing (not that I have anything against fat people it's just that last time I went to buy a suit the salesperson informed me that I might want to try shopping in the young men's department or go to Europe). Again, here as with the previous list, the emotional and moral tenor is as important as the words you chose. Many of you probably did not simply make a list but did so with a bit of cynical joy (not that I would know anything about that). This cynicism says quite a bit about us as a nation and about our self-perceptions.

America the Beautiful

So far we have discussed globalization, identity, culture, media and have looked at specific examples from China and India. While there has been a common thread running through each of the chapters, we have yet to weave it together into a common quilt (I know that weaving and quilting having nothing to do with each other, but I started with the sewing metaphor and I was going to see it through). Now is the point in the book when we begin to put everything together and what better way to pull things together than to discuss America and the American identity, since there is nothing ever divisive or controversial about America. In Chapters 4 and 6, we looked at examples of how we understand certain elements in television programs is distinct from how they are encountered by Chinese and Indian audiences, and how this is dependent upon the specific sets of cultural metaphors and inheritances. In this chapter we are going to draw out those ideas in a more direct and focused ways (no sighing, it is going to be interesting).

To go back to a point that we started with in Chapter 1, there is a direct connection between identity and culture. This means that how we understand ourselves and others is always interpreted through a cultural lens. For example, the fact that I make very little money (hint to my boss that I could use a raise) means that I am equated a lower status in contemporary America. Whenever I go to dinner parties with my wife's friends, many of whose husbands are in business, and tell them what I do, the response is always about the same: "Oh, well, that's nice" (not that I have any resentment toward this of course). The idea that how we understand who we are is always mediated by our culture was hopefully clearly, unambiguously, and poignantly demonstrated through our consideration of television programs from the American, Chinese, and Indian perspectives. What we found was that how we as citizens of the greatest country on Earth understood the images conveyed by these programs was clearly distinct from those other countries who just happen to make up one-third of the worlds population. So contrary to all those theories that place globalization as a form of cultural domination or intellectual colonialism, what we found is that rather than American television turning people into Americans, it actually turns Americans into Chinese and Indians (metaphorically of course). But before we get to how America and the American identity is understood by people in China and India, it would first be a good idea to take a good long look at ourselves.

We Americans are an extreme people. From the very inception of our country, a land founded by radical religious zealots, we have eschewed the advice of the Buddha and have seldom walked the middle path. We are a people who are either drinking a 96 oz big-gulp soda, while eating a 7-pound hamburger, supersized fries, and a 14-scoop sundae for desert (providing enough calories to sustain an entire village in Eritrea for a week), or we are having half a banana and a quarter cup of fat-free yogurt. We are a people who either spend 8 hours a day sitting on our ever-widening bums in front of electronic media, or spend 8 hours a day in the gym engaging in such intense workouts that we either throw up, pass out, or have a heart attack (usually all three, just not at the same time). We are a people who either drive cars so big that you could fit half the population of Guam in the back and with such poor gas mileage that Saudi princes get a new Rolex every time we fill up, or an environmentally conscious 50-mile-per-gallon hybrid (which we conveniently forget have toxic batteries). We are a people who bomb abortion clinics, are one of only two developed countries with the death penalty, and have the highest military spending in the world (by far), and we have the highest number of Nobel peace–prize winners. Let's not forget that we are also the developed nation with the highest number of people who believe in god, miracles, and attend church on a regular basis (and the highest number of religiously inspired theme parks, because good ol' JC loved himself a good roller coaster), along with the highest degree of scientific, technological, and medical innovation. What is particularly fantastic about us is that we can be one extreme one day and the other the next, without even pausing in the middle. Whereas the Chinese may be able to hold opposites in harmony, we push them to the furthest extremes possible (just think about the number of times the word "extreme" is used in advertising).

The fact that we, here in this nation of NASCAR, Bluegrass, and drive-through liquor stores, are a religious folk is a significant point in coming to terms with our self-understanding (follow me here, I know this seems like a sidetrack—not that I would ever do that). Bill Maher, Christopher Hitchens, Sam Harris, and their compatriots can complain all they like (and they often misunderstand the nature of religion anyway—perhaps if they took some time to actually study religion . . . well, I'll save that for another book), but no matter how much you may not want it to be true, we are a deeply religious nation. This is not to say that Pat Robertson, Jerry Falwell, Billy Graham, and their whole band of merry evangelizing men are right either when they suggest that we are a Christian nation. Rather what I am suggesting is more in line with what Robert Bellah and others have noticed; that is, there is a particular kind of religiosity built into the American psyche.[1] From the time of the founding of this country there has been a sense of America as something different, something special; it is a new Zion, a city on a hill, the light of the world, or whatever other biblical allusion you would like to throw in there. What this means is that regardless of whether we actually go to church or synagogue, we as Americans are a chosen people who are called to be the guide to all the lesser nations in the world (and that would be all of them). The reason I bring this up, other than the fact that I find religion fascinating, is that it provides us with an interesting trope (good word) for understanding American self-understanding and our cultural products. On one side, we have us as a chosen people better than all of the rest, but the flipside of this religious consciousness, particularly when we do not live up to this ideal (which is most of the time since it is a fairly high bar) is judgment, damnation, and ultimately the apocalypse. But before we start running from the four horsemen, let's spend a minute with the glories of heaven.

Of Saints

The positive side of the American identity is, well, very positive. When we are in our mode as chosen people we celebrate, extol, glorify, laud, and praise ourselves to no end. America is THE land of freedom, THE land of liberty, THE land of Democracy, THE land of truth, THE land of justice, and THE land of super-value meals. As the citizens of this country, we then are the bearers of all of these things. This aspect of America does admittedly tend to be a bit more common among those people residing in states that appear red on all of those funny, interactive political maps pulled out during elections. To drive through Dixie or middle America is to find American flags flying proudly in the wind, yellow ribbons tied around trees, the twang of country music stars flowing from the radio singing about the glory of America, and walking into Waffle Houses open even at 3 a.m. in the morning when you are so inebriated that you cannot sit upright in the booth and the waitress still calls you sweetheart (not that this ever happened). While the stereotype of the patriotic types who celebrate America living outside the coasts may have some degree of truth, this consciousness is not limited to people with relatives named Junior, Zeik, or Beulah. Shows like CSI, CSI New York, CSI Miami, CSI Cincinnati (that one did not make the cut for some reason), Law and Order, Law and Order: SVU, NCIS, and every other crime drama that populates the channels each in their own way celebrates the Americanness of truth, justice, and liberty. Almost every sitcom, no matter how dysfunctional the characters may be and, sometimes because of it, demonstrates that the American dream is possible for anyone. This is all to say that the idea that we Americans are a chosen people has a significant place in our consciousness, television programming, and self-understanding.

In many ways, it is this positive vision that we offer to the world. The positive vision of ourselves is like the fancy clothes that we put on to try to make ourselves look good when we go out with all of the other nations. We want to be the popular nation, the cool nation, and the nation that all the other countries want to be. America when it's out on a Saturday night walks with a certain swagger and shake of the hips that allures and teases all the other countries. But much like the popular girl who on the outside appears fashionable, pretty, calm, and confident, but on the inside is an emotional and psychological train wreck and just uses the external form to cover over deep insecurities (sometimes stereotypes are true), America also, when alone in our room with ourselves, has deep-rooted self-doubt and negative feelings.

And Sinners

The alternative vision of ourselves as Americans, the one that we encounter when we watch many contemporary television programs, is the inverse of our sense of ourselves as chosen; it is (again to get biblical on you) our fallenness. This negative self-evaluation that we carry as one of our dominant social metaphors should have become fairly clear as we went through the programs in Chapters 4 and 6. Time and again, ideas of emptiness, meaninglessness, purposelessness, social decay, suburban despair, moral lassitude, narcissism, and to use a word that I made up in a previous chapter, our own craptacularness, were given voice and image. Though nothing new, the idea that we have of our own country and ourselves as fallen, broken, or at least on the wrong path, has increased significantly over the last generation. If you were to go onto Amazon.

com and type in the word America into the book search the majority of
the first two pages of results would be about how America
is bad, wrong, falling apart, decaying, imploding, or ending. Some
representative titles include, *The End of America*,[2] *Idiot America*,[3]
America Alone: The End of the World As We Know It,[4] *Unscientific
America: How Scientific Illiteracy Threatens our Future*,[5] and of course
the somewhat less despairing but equally cynical books by Jon Stewart[6]
and Stephen Colbert.[7] One fascinating point about these books is that
they are written by Americans and intended largely for American
audiences. While this particular list is composed of primarily liberal
authors, the invective and vitriol is no less severe from the opposite end
of the social and political spectrum (even if it is for different reasons
that somehow always get linked back to homosexuality—maybe its just
me, but it seems that right-wing conservatives spend more time thinking about gay sex than gay men). When you have Rush Limbaugh
and Bill Maher agreeing on something, then you know there must be a
problem.

It is strange to think that a country like ours, which has so much
patriotism and pride and a sense of itself as chosen for a special mission,
could also be so despairing and convinced about its own end—unless of
course it makes perfect sense. To return to the point that us good ol' boys
are deeply religious people (regardless of our beliefs), part of this
religiosity is our sense of our own end or, to use religious language, the
apocalypse. Anyone who has spent any time in the South during the
winter will know exactly what I mean. I lived in Tennessee for a couple
of years, and during my first winter there, on a day that seemed like any
other, I went over to the local Harris Teeter (the Piggly Wiggly, and Win
Dixie were a bit too far) to pick up some groceries. My car was one of
three in what was usually a crowded parking lot. When I walked inside
it looked as though there had been a soccer riot in the aisles—there was
no bread, milk, eggs, or bottled water to be found in the entire store.
When I asked the Southern belle at the check-out counter, she replied
(and here you have to try to imagine a cloyingly sweet Southern drawl)
"Well, didn'cha hear? There might right be a full inch or more of snow
tonight." My reply, having lived in Montreal for 5 years previous to this
was, "Right . . . and . . . " To which I received a big smile and a bat of the
eyelashes (charming to be sure, but somewhat less than helpful). I quickly

came to realize that any time there was even the possibility of snow, sleet, ice, or even a particularly heavy rain storm, and occasionally even a strong breeze, the entire city would go out shopping for the apocalypse—because if the end is coming you better have yourself some milk and cookies waiting for JC. The significance of this story, beyond the fact that it always makes me laugh, is that it speaks to a type of consciousness built into the American psyche that is always aware of judgment, and our shortcomings/sins as a nation and people.

This intense sense of self-judgment that is built into our cultural psyche assumes many guises. We have accused ourselves of being taken over by technology and becoming slaves to machinery, of losing our sense of morality, of intense narcissism, of leading empty and vapid lives, of having no sense of purpose, and of being greedy and selfish, and of course of being ignorant, stupid, culturally insensitive, aggressive, and fat (I prefer big-boned). Many of these things are rooted in our own cultural history and have complex origins that we cannot get into at this point (yet another future book—maybe I should quite my day job). Regardless of the origin of these rather negative self-evaluations, they are such common metaphors in American culture that they get continually represented in our culture particularly in our media. This point should have been abundantly clear in Chapters 4 and 6 where we time and again saw programs either based on, playing upon, or embodying these negative cultural stereotypes. Whether it is the dysfunctional relationships of *Friends*, the bizarre, meaningless cultural collage of *Lost*, or the narcissistic desire to be a special in *Heroes*, we are encountering a sense of ourselves that is less flattering than spandex on an average American.

What we arrive at when we consider how we conceive of our own nation and our identities as citizens of that nation is a very American form of categorical opposites that fits perfectly with our all or nothing, win or lose, right or wrong, regular or extra crispy sense of the world. Our great homeland and we, the religiously inspired denizens of this blessed new Zion, is either heaven or hell, and we are either sinners or saints. Our media plays upon this dichotomy to such a degree that we tend not to even recognize it, because it is part of who we are. One of my favorite Germans (minus the whole tacit support of the Nazi party thing), Heidegger, once said that we have the most difficult time seeing what is ready at hand (actually it would have been far more confusing than that and in German, but I didn't want to overtax you). His point, which fits nicely with a major point of this book, is that we tend not to notice the world around us because we are part of it, just as we tend not to notice our cultural metaphors and background because they partly compose our identity. But just as our identity as Americans is tied in with our culture, the perception of our identity by others is also tied into theirs, and as we saw in the previous chapters, this can be quite different than our own. So now it is time to look at us from other perspectives, ones that do not include the saint or the sinner.

Through the Eyes of Another

When we begin to look at how we are viewed through the eyes of others, the first thing that we have to remember is that as was discussed in Chapter 3 and 5, they are beginning from a distinct cultural background in which our conceptual categories may not even make sense. So whereas we may think that the average Chinese person would think of Americans as bad people, this would not even make sense to the average Chinese person who does not operate from a position of moral dichotomies (remember right and wrong rather than right or wrong— if you correctly remembered this point, reward yourself with Fun Dip—who doesn't pore sugar on a pure-sugar stick). Another important point is that there is an significant distinction between America and Americans, something that was made quite clear during the Bush years in which the country was universally hated, but the people were just strongly disliked. While the opinions of people and the place do tend to be close to one another, luckily we usually seem to always win out over our much-maligned nation, except in one important case that we will consider in a minute.

The Pew Research Center has a Global Attitudes Project that measures the favorability of Americans in the eyes of different nations as well as things like the favorability of the president, peoples opinions on the war on terror, and our consideration of other nations interests (don't worry, it's not as bad as you think). If you look at these surveys a few fascinating points arise. First, and completely unrelated to the topic at hand but still rather amusing, Kenyans have a higher favorability rating of us than we do of ourselves (I would imagine Obama's Kenyan heritage may have a small influence here). More importantly, right behind Canada, Britain, and France (it's a myth that the French don't like us—they just don't like nutty right-wing Republicans who pour French wine into gutters, but then who does), India has one of the highest favorability ratings of the United States coming in at 73%. This is no doubt aided by the fact that 81% of Indians believe that we have high regard for other countries interests and 82% support our efforts against terrorism. This is perhaps not terribly surprising coming from a country with which we recently signed a nuclear treaty and which is also fighting Islamic terrorists. When we hop north-east across the Himalayas we find a very different picture. Coming in just above Egypt and Jordan, only 42% of Chinese people surveyed have a favorable opinion of Americans. Interestingly, China is also one of the only countries on the survey for which America is more favorable than Americans, with the nation receiving a 47% favorable rating (still not rave reviews but slightly better).[8]

The Pew surveys are interesting for a number of reasons. Beyond the fact that they inform us where we should not wear American flags while traveling (Turkey, Pakistan, and the Palestinian territories may not be the best choices), they help us get a vague sense of the affective encounter with the American identity. For our purposes, however, the point that sticks out more than any other is that in China, where American television programming is consumed more readily than rice, the affective encounter is fairly negative, whereas in India, where American programming is less popular, the encounter is quite positive. The obvious conclusion to draw from this would be that the more people watch our programs, the less they like us, except of course this commits countless formal and informal logical fallacies. As I am sure you remember from one of your social science classes, correlation does not mean causation—just because two things are related does not mean that one causes the other. This point is proven by the fact that Canadians and Brits who consume more American media than any other countries maintain very positive evaluations of both America and Americans (although as someone who lived in Canada for five years I quickly came to realize that making fun of Americans was a favored Canadian pastime—even more so than curling). Similarly, of course, low viewing levels of American television does not guarantee a high favorability rating. I am fairly sure that the majority of people living in the disputed Palestinian territories do not spend their days watching American TV, and our favorability rating there is a not-too-surprising 20%.

If the favorability rating of the America in the eyes of China and India points to anything, it is that there is not a direct relationship between watching American television programming and ideas about America and the American identity. This highlights a theme that has been present throughout this book, that television programming once it leaves its culture of origin becomes a multivocal medium onto which projected is the cultural metaphors and values of those encountering it. The person watching bootleg DVDs in Nanjing, China, does not think that everyone in America is like the people on the *Lost* island, at least not as we view them (although it would be far more entertaining if they were), nor do they want to be like us by virtue of watching these shows. Similarly, someone living in Mysore, India, watching *The OC* is not seeing the Orange County that we know (since we all have fancy beach homes there) and does not try to emulate us, at least not as we understand ourselves. Our friends in Nanjing and Mysore are encountering programs that are viewed through their own distinct cultural lenses, and their choices about what to see, say far more about their own background, culture, social location, and nation than they do about America or Americans.

Globalization Redux

This brings us back to another point that we discussed in the first chapter, globalization. If you can remember that far back (I have trouble with what I did yesterday, but hopefully you are holding up better than I am), one of the theories of globalization we discussed was Americanization or the idea that globalization is nothing more than a form of American economic, political, and cultural imperialism. The lefties over at Berkley are always holding rallies and beating on drums to protest the opening of a new McDonald's, Starbucks, KFC, Gap, Reebok Store, or whatever corporate giant is the most evil on that day, in some developing nation and claiming that it will destroy their native culture (I have on numerous occasions tried to point out that it is a bit ironically racist for a bunch of White folks to hold rallies to protect the non-white folks from the White folks, but my insight was unappreciated). What we have seen, however, is that rather than American cultural products making foreign cultures like America, they are read through the local culture and become something completely different. This is to say that American programming does not make other cultures more like us (in the sense of similarity), nor, as the Pew surveys point out, does it make them like us (in the sense of appreciation). Rather, it is a space for people from other cultures to project themselves, their ideas, and their cultural metaphors onto American images.

American television programming does not serve as a major corrupting influence on other cultures (we are spectacular, but we can't do everything), nor does it necessarily inform other cultures' understanding of us as Americans. It does, however, serve as a fascinating starting point for intercultural communication—a point that we will take up in the next, and final, chapter (go get your Kleenex ready, we are almost at an end, and I know there will be tears when we say goodbye). But before we move on to the final piece of this puzzle, we still need to spend a bit more time thinking about the American identity through the eyes of others. In particular, once we give up the idea that American television programming is giving India and China a vision of us as Americans, and begin to realize that it is a multivocal canvas onto which these cultures project and represent themselves, we begin to arrive at a different understanding of what they are seeing. In the end, who we are to them is a combination of their own cultural backgrounds, informed by the stuff we discussed in Chapters 3 and 5, along with the news, information, and education they receive about us. To give you an example, if you ask the average American their idea of Chinese people, they will usually say things like Chinese food and Communists, two things that reflect their own lifeworld (ubiquitous Chinese restaurants) and what they hear/read/see on the news (damn Communists).

When we turn to China and see how wildly popular American programming is, our 40-percent approval rating does not seem to make much sense. If, however, you begin to watch Chinese TV (there is one coma-inducing English-language channel on China Central Television that might as well have been in Chinese because my mind shut down after about 2 minutes of watching it), or reading their news sources, all of which, remember, are tightly stated controlled, the 40-percent approval rating begins to make sense. Other than the Russian newspaper *Pravda*, which publishes such virulent yet amusing stories about America as "America's Economy Collapses," "Missile Defense System: Fraud of the Century," and "Two Russian Nuclear Subs Make US Tremble with Fear," few countries' media is as anti-American as China. While more subtle than *Pravda*, the Chinese news agencies often portray America as against China, as competitors, as a threat to their society or well-being, as, well, America. This, is of course, not one sided since our media, although not to the same degree, plies in the same type of ideas (some—Fox News—more than others). In the end, if the majority of information you are receiving about another people or nation is that they are opposed to your way of life and it is you versus them, it is terribly unlikely that you will have a particularly high opinion of them (unless of course you have the self-esteem of a 14-year-old girl, in which case you may just agree with them).

If we move from the land of pandas to the land of elephants, a very different idea of America and the American identity emerges. To the average Indian, as they will readily tell you on the street time and again, and again, and again, and again, America is a "very, very good place." This positive vision of our great land is in large measure due to the Indian cultural background, which with its emphasis on universality, democracy, and its love of fried foods is inherently more amenable to the American way of life, combined with the sources of information available. In the case of India, the media is free from state control, and tends, particularly since the 1990s, to present a fairly positive view of America as a friend to India and sharing in common interests (aka killing Muslim terrorists). Another piece that serves to influence the Indian perspective on America and Americans is that every single person you speak to in India seems to have an uncle, cousin, brother, friend, friend of a cousin, uncle of a roommate, cricket teammate, pen pal, or schoolmate from second grade living in or having just come back from living in the United States. The majority of the stories they hear are of opportunity, wealth, and a Starbucks on every corner (personally I prefer Indian Coffee House but that is in part because coffee only costs 20 cents and I'll take a 1-dollar dosa over a 7-dollar piece of coffee cake any day). Collectively, the cultural affinity, positive portrayal in news and educational sources, and somewhat embellished first-hand accounts almost make us seem like Zion that we (sometimes) know we are.

The Chinese and Indians have very different views of America and the American identity that are conditioned by their own cultural backgrounds and their sources of news and information. A similar point can be made for any other country as well, but what is particularly interesting about India and China is that when looked at together they exhibit a particularly American quality: a black or white, this or that, right or wrong, top or bottom, aisle or window, kind of contrast. India leans toward the metaphor of chosenness while China lines up with the opposite of fallenness. Of course, neither of these cultures would put this in biblical language (I suppose in India it may be more like Pandavas vs Kauravas, while in China it would be Mao vs Kuomintang, but again the either/or consciousness does not really hold), but the idea remains the same. On one side, we have a fairly positive evaluation that embraces aspects of American culture and identity, while, on the other, you have a negative evaluation that views the United States and its citizens as opponents or competitors. An interesting example of the Chinese perspective on America was readily found in the Chinese print propaganda (aka newspapers) during the Beijing Olympics. All of the papers were rife with stories about how it is the end of the American century and the beginning of the rise of China, something that sounds rather similar to the titles of the books from the amazon.com search (maybe the Republicans are right about all of those lefties being Communists). These positive or negative views do not, however, necessarily correlate to an understanding of America.

Television as a multivocal medium, once it crosses cultural boundaries, onto which foreign cultural metaphors, ideas, and stereotypes can be projected, can help us understand India and China's encounter of the American identity (and for that matter any other country as well). Just as American television programs become Chinese or Indian once they cross over into the respective countries, so too do all cultural products and cultural identities. To put this another way the American identity in China and India is the Chinese or Indian interpretation of the American identity, which may well have little relationship to the American version of the American identity (which may be a good thing). So, when the Chinese dislike us or the Indians like us, we cannot take much credit for either, since they are ultimately responding to something other than us. America's greatest gift to the world, fast food, can help provide a useful example. If you were to travel through India and find yourself hankering for that bastion American culture that is proudly marked by the glowing golden arches, you are in for a bit of a shock. Instead of hamburgers you will find mutton burgers (the sacred cow thing makes eating beef somewhat less than popular), accompanied by interesting vegetarian options such as the aloo tikki burger (don't worry, you can still get fries). If while trekking the great wall you found yourself desperate for some biscuits and mashed potatoes and decided to track down Colonel Sanders, one of the first things you would find on the menu, more prominent than original or extra crispy are the Chinese chicken wings that are common here at all take-out Chinese restaurants. These two restaurants are McDonald's and KFC, and yet they are the Indian and Chinese interpretations of these things. In the end, it is a little bit of us and little bit of them.

Come Together Right Now Over Me

This entire discussion of the encounter and understanding of the American identity has likely raised the ire of countless philosophical types who are irritably pacing back and forth, wringing their hands, wondering how I can so blithely gloss over such significant issues as perception, reality, and truth. They are standing there, hair all a mess, in their threadbare tweed jackets with the patches on the elbows, softly muttering about the Platonic notion of ideal types, Hegel's concept of "das ding an sich," or perhaps Foucault's notion of subject positions (anyone who knows what all of these are wins a prize). With due respect to my philosophically inclined colleagues, I think I am going to see their Plato, Hegel, and Foucault, and raise them a Wittgenstein, who in his abstruse and much-misunderstood work *Tractatus Logico-Philosophicus* (how could it not be misunderstood with a name like that) suggests that "The world is all that is the case."[9] This somewhat reclusive, mentally unstable, yet brilliant, man (these characteristics do seem to go together) brings us back to a point that we discussed in the beginning of the book. Rather than imposing a theory upon what we are studying, we are instead going to look and see what we find. This is to say that theories about cultural perceptions, identity structure, and the meaning of meaning are somewhat less important (at least for our purposes) than the lived lives and experiences of actual people (there seems to be an inverse correlation between years spent in university settings and capacity to fully function in society—but that is a topic for yet another book).

Our concern in this book, and in a broader sense in the fields of media and cultural studies, is not to make the world more complicated by adding layer upon layer of theories of globalization, culture, identity, and media, but rather to help clarify these ideas. In the words of our friend Wittgenstein (albeit I seriously doubt he would have been all that much fun to hang out with), the goal of any study should be the clarification of language and thought. This is to say that when we are trying to understand how America is viewed through the eyes of China and India, the question of which American identity is real is less significant than which one is experienced as real. That might not have helped; let's try this another way. Imagine you have a situation in which a boy named Ludwig grew up in such a way that he misunderstood the word "chair" to refer to cake (who doesn't love cake). If we were to meet Ludwig at some point and ask him to have a seat on the chair, he would certainly cast a curious glance our way (unless of course he enjoys sitting on cake, which admittedly seems as though it could be vaguely amusing). We may come to realize that Ludwig has the "wrong" understanding of the word chair, but to him his understanding is as real as our own. His favorite kind of chair is funfeti with chocolate icing; his mom bakes him a chair every year on his birthday, and one time when he was 5 he ate his sister's chair and got grounded for a week (it was worth it). This is, of course, a linguistic mistake, but it helps us understand something about the encounter of identity.

Whenever we encounter another person, we are not reacting to the person as they are, but rather to the person as we understand them, and this understanding is as real to us as their own self-understanding is to them. If you were to come across someone and saw them wearing stilettos, a skirt so short that it looks as though a tube top migrated South, a shirt that would make the Pope blush, and enough makeup to keep Bobbi Brown in business for the next decade, you might assume this person was in the same line of work as Mary Magdalene and Mata Hari. If you were to approach her and ask her about her services (not to assume anything about you of course), you may well receive a slap across the face since this Britney Spears/Paris Hilton/Sex and the City–inspired woman was simply going out on a Saturday night to meet her friends for drinks. When you approached her, your assumption about her identity was as real to you as was her own belief, that she looked good (there is no accounting for taste). Just as this occurs on an individual level, so too does it occur on a cultural level. So, the perception of the American identity that is carried by people from China, India, or for that matter, any other nation, is as real to them as our is to ourselves. This creates a fascinating situation in which when people from different cultures try to talk to one another, they are for the most part not talking to one another; they are instead talking to their own idea of the other (something also common in relationships—Woman: "Do you want to go out with my friends, tonight?" Man: "No, I am tired, I think I will stay in." Woman: "I knew you hate my friends." Man: "No, I am just tired." Woman: "You've always hated them, you are so mean." Man: "I, but, I, uh, um, I . . . "). This problem of intercultural communication will be the focus of the final chapter, but before we get there let's look at one more aspect of identity.

As we discussed all the way back in Chapter 1, identities are fluid, flexible, and continually changing, and this is in large measure related to the culture in which they are located. Anyone who has been around (or have themselves been) a first-year college student will know exactly what I mean. Once students arrive at college and are exposed to new cultures and ways of being, they begin to try on new identities more rapidly than brides-to-be try on dresses at a designer sample sale. You have the stoner one week, the scholar the next, the party kid the week after, and the jock perhaps the week after that; maybe there is a little Buddhist period tossed in, and let's not forget the gender and sexuality issues, but of course that was just that one time when you were really drunk. The ability to cycle through all of the identity types portrayed by John Hughes in the Breakfast Club is allowed for by the culture in which these students find themselves—one that encourages openness and exploration. Whether or not there is something of us that remains over time and place, our identities are always open to renegotiation. As time moves forward (assuming a linear perspective on time, which as you know I reject), and America, China, and India, all continue to change and develop, the meaning of the American identity to all three of them will continue to change along with it. Because of this our ability to understand the relationship between identity, culture, media, and communication is more important than the specific content of this relationship at any one time.

The end draws near (all of the readers in Nashville have just put down the book and run to the grocery store so they can bake cookies for Jesus). But before we say our final goodbyes, we have one more chapter to go. So hold off on the tears (don't worry, we can keep in touch over facebook) and get ready to learn how to communicate—'cause its always a good idea to know how to talk good.

Notes

1. Bellah, Robert N. *Beyond Belief: Essays on Religion in a Post-Traditionalist World.* University of California Press, 1991.
2. Wolf, Naomi. *The End of America: Letter of Warning to a Young Patriot.* 1st ed. Chelsea Green Publishing, 2007.
3. Pierce, Charles P. *Idiot America: How Stupidity Became a Virtue in the Land of the Free.* Doubleday, 2009.
4. Steyn, Mark. *America Alone: The End of the World as We Know It.* Regnery Publishing, 2008.
5. Mooney, Chris, and Sheril Kirshenbaum. *Unscientific America: How Scientific Illiteracy Threatens Our Future.* Basic Books, 2009.
6. Stewart, Jon, and The Writers of The Daily Show. *The Daily Show with Jon Stewart Presents America (The Book) Teacher's Edition: A Citizen's Guide to Democracy Inaction.* Tch. Grand Central Publishing, 2006.
7. Colbert, Stephen. *I Am America.* 1st ed. Grand Central Publishing, 2007.
8. "Chart of Opinion of the United States in 2009— Pew Global Attitudes Project Key Indicators Database." http://pewglobal.org/database
9. Wittgenstein, Ludwig. *Tractatus Logico-Philosophicus.* Cosimo Classics, 2007.

Suggestions for Further Reading

Bellah, Robert N. *Beyond Belief: Essays on Religion in a Post-Traditionalist World.* University of California Press, 1991.
Colbert, Stephen. *I Am America.* 1st ed. Grand Central Publishing, 2007.
Ehrenreich, Barbara. *Nickel and Dimed: On (Not) Getting by in America.* Reprint. Holt Paperbacks, 2008.

Mooney, Chris, and Sheril Kirshenbaum. *Unscientific America: How Scientific Illiteracy Threatens Our Future.* Basic Books, 2009.

Pierce, Charles P. *Idiot America: How Stupidity Became a Virtue in the Land of the Free.* Doubleday, 2009.

Stewart, Jon, and The Writers of The Daily Show. *The Daily Show with Jon Stewart Presents America (The Book) Teacher's Edition: A Citizen's Guide to Democracy Inaction.* Tch. Grand Central Publishing, 2006.

Steyn, Mark. *America Alone: The End of the World as We Know It.* Regnery Publishing, 2008.

Wittgenstein, Ludwig. *Tractatus Logico-Philosophicus.* Cosimo Classics, 2007.

Wolf, Naomi. *The End of America: Letter of Warning to a Young Patriot.* 1st ed. Chelsea Green Publishing, 2007.

8

Ignore Your Mother, Talk to Strangers

Exercise #6

I feel as though some exercise may be good today. I am a bit stressed; this is the second time I am starting this chapter, since the first time I tried, which ever god in the Hindu pantheon is responsible for technology decided to mock me by erasing my file. I am going to have to sick Durga on him. Technology-inspired rage aside, we still have work to do and this time you need to go find yourself a partner. It does not really matter much who you choose. A roommate; friend; significant other; local Congressman; crazy, homeless guy who is always predicting the end of the world; the cute barista at Starbucks that you having been eyeing but are to shy to talk to, or, if all else fails, your mom (she misses you—you really should call more often).

(While you find your partner I am going to repeatedly kick my computer)

Okay, I am starting to feel a bit better, although I somehow think that kicking my computer may well have made it even more likely I will lose files. Now that I have damaged my foot, and you have found a partner, lets get started. I want you to find a few different examples of modern art (MOMA has an excellent free database moma.org). It does not really matter what you pick, and in this case the more abstract or curious the better. Do not talk to your partner about what you are choosing; you will get to the discussion section later. For now, just select the works. Once they are chosen, stare at them for a few minutes and then both you and your partner should write down what you see, encounter, understand, think about these modern marvels.

(Take your time, I am on my way to staples to buy a flash drive, zip drive, external hard drive, and any other means of backing up my files I can find)

Now that you have made your lists, I want you to compare what you wrote. Did one of you see a brilliant work of art that reveals the deepest truths of the universe, while the other just saw a black dot on white canvas? Did one of you feel a chill run down your spine as you encountered something truly profound, while the most intense experience for the other person was regret for having agreed to do this. Was one of you sure that you knew exactly what the artist was trying to convey, while the only thing the other person was sure of was that the artist was doing drugs. Did you look at the same thing and see/experience something completely different? Probably yes. Now that you have written about what you see, I want you to try something a bit more difficult (come one, you can do it, just one more rep, almost there, you got this ...) I want you to take back what you wrote, look it over, and figure out why you encountered and understood the art the way you did.

(In the mean time I will be trying to figure out how all the techno crap I just bought works)

Was this task more difficult? For the most part as we go about our lives we just act and respond to people and things without stopping to think about or reflect on what we are seeing or doing. If that is the case, and we for the most part do not even now how or why we see and react to things the way we do, how can we be expected to understand how other people encounter the same things? If we do not understand how ourselves or others encounter the world how can we be expected to communicate about it? Why must I ask so many questions? Let's find out.

Can We Talk?

We have covered a good bit of ground in a short time. We have examined the ideas of globalization, culture, and identity, have traveled through China and India (or at least I did—you got to remain in the comfort of your homes while I got jet lag, dysentery, and some curious rash that won't seem to go away), and watched countless hours of television. What we have arrived at so far is a vision in which identity and culture are inexorably intertwined, cultural products become multivocal and open to renegotiation once they cross cultural boundaries, and in which television does not "Americanize" foreign audiences but rather becomes "foreignized" or maybe "nativized" (or whatever word you choose to make up) when it is encountered by other cultures. As we saw in the last chapter, what this means is that the whoness and whatness (I am all about making up words in this chapter) of who and what we are is quite different for us than it is for Chinese and Indian audiences and that consumption of American television programs does not correlate to a better (or worse) opinion or understanding of the American identity. While this may be somewhat encouraging considering the resoundingly negative cultural metaphors that we encounter in our television programming (not that we do not come by it honestly, since this is the only country where you can go to a drive-through liquor store, buy a shotgun at Wal-Mart, and then head out hunting in your 12-mpg pickup truck while listening to Rush Limbaugh rail against the dangers of civil and human rights), it does present an interesting problem and opportunity for intercultural communication.

If people in China and India came to understand us as we understand ourselves through out television programming (which they do not), or even (and here I want all you antiglobalization types to skip the next line so that you do not get all worked up and start a drum circle or protest) were they to be "Americanized" through cultural imperialism, the possibility for intercultural communication would actually be increased. To be clear (so as to avoid unnecessary hate mail, so that there is more room for bills and catalogs in my mail box) I am not saying Americanization of the world is a good thing, only that, were it the case (god forbid, since I have no idea why we would want Communist China with its horrible record on human rights, no democratic process, massive oppression of its own population, to be more like us), it would provide a baseline of understanding for communication. Without some type of common starting point, and with distinct cultural backgrounds, and metaphors, the ability to communicate and understand one another becomes far more challenging. The other side of this is that misunderstanding can be a wonderful thing, in that if we both misunderstand the same thing together, if we clarify why we understand it the way we do to ourselves and to the other person, a deep and thorough understanding can emerge. This is to say that perhaps the fact that the American identity is received in different ways by Chinese and Indian television audiences than it is by us may actually be useful since it can serve as a point of contact, dialogue, and eventual understanding. Yes, I know this seems ironically confusing considering we are discussing understanding, but we have the rest of the chapter to figure it out.

Before we look at television's possible role in intercultural communication let's first spend some time discussing what this even means (its usually good to know what you are talking about—I don't, but I hear from other people that it can be useful). The first thing that we have to realize is that much like culture, identity, and globalization, there are countless takes on the meaning, theory, method, and practice of intercultural communication. Essays, articles, and books on this topic range from discussions of how history and identity are tied into communication,[1] to issues in business communications,[2] to the international best-selling page turner "Bilingual Communication in Organizational Settings: Aspects of the Canadian Case"[3] (I can almost hear the doors slam as you all rush out to pick up a copy for yourself). Any number of issues can be lumped under the term *intercultural communication*, from the broad philosophical discussion of the nature of language to the more arcane examination of a particular communication form in a recently discovered tribe in a crater in the jungles of Papua New Guinea (I think there are more anthropologists in New Guinea at this point than tribesmen). We will, however, be discussing none of these things.

Much like in the early chapters in the book where we (it is funny that I keep saying we being that I am the one making all the decisions, but much like life I try to provide at least the illusion of control) decided to eschew theory in favor of looking and seeing what we find, we will once again walk this path. We could discuss the idea of universal grammar, high- and low-context languages, individualist versus collectivist cultures, emic and etic characteristic, and all kinds of other fun academic jargon, but in the end we would just end up fitting a phenomenon into our theory. This is, of course, far more convenient, but we Americans are a diligent and hard-working people (insert laughter here), so we will leave the laziness for the French (insert angry croissant throwing here) and try a different approach. Rather than looking at how we are different, we are instead going to look at what happens when people with different cultural backgrounds or worldviews come together.

Mission Control: We Have Contact

The approach we are going to take in this section is going to find help from a rather unlikely source. Instead of turning to a linguist, expert in communications, or cultural theorist, we are going to look to a retired professor of physics and religion (follow me here, I promise I am not losing it . . . quite yet). Ian Barbour, who is the preeminent scholar in the field of religion and science, once suggested that there are four principle modes of encounter between these two fields: conflict, independence, dialogue, and integration. We will focus on the first three (integration of cultures is a bit far off, so we can put it to the side for now). The interaction between science and religion provides an excellent model for our discussion of intercultural communication because they are normally perceived as opposing worldviews (this position is actually incorrect and leads to people publishing pointless tirades about the horrors of religion and starting atheists societies that seem ironically religious, but we will ignore all that for now). Barbour's basic point is that since worldviews/cultures are all encompassing, when they come into contact with one another there is no choice but to address the relationship.[4] If you and I are in a room together with an object and I say that it is a red chair, and you say if is a garden gnome, there is obviously a point that needs to be addressed (and perhaps one of us may need some counseling).

I Am Right. No, I Am Right. No, No, I Am Right, No, No, No I Am Right . . .

The first possible mode of intercultural communication is simple enough, conflict (something that we are all abundantly good at). In this mode of contact when people from different cultures come together the interaction would look something like this: "I am right," "No, I am right." "No, no, I am right and your are wrong." "No, no, no, I am right and you are wrong." "You are a jerk." "Who are you calling a jerk?" "Your mother."

"Oh, so you are going to bring her into this. Well, your mother is so fat that last time she laid out on the beach Greenpeace dragged her back into the water." Perhaps, it would not quite reach the point of mother jokes (as funny as they may be), but you should get the basic idea. If I view *Lost* as a commentary on the breakdown of meaning in the West, and you view *Lost* as a commentary on the dynamic nature of life and death and we are both intransigent in our positions, then there is no dialogue or communication. The danger with conflict is that disagreement can lead to imposition, and in this case the stronger party often wins.

The conflict model of intercultural communication relates back to the idea of globalization as Americanization, where American cultural products take on and replace those from other countries. It is as though America was a bully with a big stick walking around telling all the kids on the playground that he is the best and they have to agree with everything he says (although much like with a schoolyard bully, it is done out of fear and with resentment—a positive grounding for any relationship). The problem with this mode of communication is that, as we have previously discussed, people are not passive receptors of information and one worldview or culture cannot simply be imposed upon another—no matter how much force you use (albeit the idea of waterboarding someone to get them to agree with your interpretation of *Lost* is at least vaguely amusing—and completely wrong of course).

The conflict model, while often viewed as the most common if not inevitable model of communication between people with competing viewpoints, is neither common nor inevitable, it only appears so. When Dick Cheney and Osama Bin Laden put out their loving messages to the world (not that I would ever put them in the same category—although neither one of them seems to have a working heart), as much as they would like to, they are not enforcing their message upon anyone. They are more like the well-paid lobbyists that Cheney is so fond of; they may strongly suggest something, but since people are active interpreters of information and participant in their culture, it is never simply received or recorded. To go back to our primary focus, when American television is broadcast in India, China, or any other country it is not being enforced upon the viewers but rather encountered by them and renegotiated— but we will get to that in a minute (patience is a virtue—unless you are in a burning building, or a sinking car, being attacked by a bear, or basically any emergency situation).

I'd Like to Teach the World to Sing in Perfect Harmony

The next model of intercultural communication is that of independence. I think the best way to understand this is to imagine that Coke commercial from the 80s where all of the perfectly coordinated children of every imaginable ethnicity were walking over the flowering meadow, with the sun shining over head singing, "I'd like to teach the world to sing in perfect harmony . . . " (this ad was only slightly less cloying than the diabetes-inducing, high-fructose corn syrup–laden, brown substance that was being advertised). Now do not get me wrong; I have nothing against everyone coming together and celebrating their difference in one giant I'm-okay-you-are-okay love fest, I am just not completely sure how well it would work (the school I work at actually has a diversity coordinator—I am not exactly sure what she does, but I always like to imagine that she stands at the door when the kids walk in and point to them one at a time saying, "And today you will be Chinese, and you Dominican, and you Bhutanese, and you a Sunni Muslim . . . ") In terms of dialogue and communication, what this would mean is that each cultural message is equally correct, equally respected, and equally valued. Even if we grant the possibility that this could happen (about as likely a Taliban float at a gay-pride parade), a deep philosophical problem remains.

If we were only talking about something as simple as some your favorite flavor of ice cream, saying that all choices are equally good may be simple enough (albeit it would be pretty funny to see a couple of hippies thrown down over Cherry Garcia vs Phish Food). When we are talking about the interaction between cultures, however, much more is at stake. If you say that the world was created in six days by some invisible guy who got tired and need a day off to rest when he was done, and I say that it was actually a product of a god who assumed the form of a tortoise spinning on its back, we cannot simply agree to disagree. We are both making fundamental claims about the nature of the cosmos, which, if one were true, would completely and totally invalidate the other person's sense of the world (which surprisingly makes some people uncomfortable). When we are faced with fundamental questions of truth, time, being, and meaning, the kind of stuff that makes up culture and also our identity (remember how they are related?), it is not as simple as just saying that everything is equally true or good.

Television programs, as multivocal mediums, do allow for distinct encounters when they are moved beyond their cultural boundaries. That said, if these distinct encounters are brought together they do not comfortably coexist. It is one thing for me to have an interpretation of *The OC* as a show about the cultural decay, narcissism, and decadence of America, and someone from India to see it as a representation of the American dream (in the positive sense). If, however, we want to talk to one another about *The OC* (because whenever I meet people from other countries my first topic of conversation is painfully stereotyped teen melodramas) these differing interpretations will prove problematic because they draw upon distinct cultural metaphors and backgrounds. While this may not serve as the basis for the next major war (although I suppose you never know since the Iraq war was started on less substantial grounds), it does lead to a kind of cognitive dissonance that we do not simply accept. Again, as active interpreters of our world, we do not simply sit idly by and say, "Oh, isn't that nice that other people see things differently than me. I accept them exactly as they are. Everything is fine," unless of course we are heavily medicated on one of the three musketeers of American mood-altering drugs: Zoloft, Paxil, and Prozac, which most of us are.

We Need to Talk

If conflict does not work, and independence is not a possibility, what are we left with—say it with me now, dialogue. In one sense this may seem obvious and simple enough; we talk to each other and discuss things all the time, so why would this be any different for intercultural communication. However, in truth, we for the most part talk at each other and already have our minds made up (this should be abundantly clear to anyone who has ever been in any form of romantic relationship). Imagine this scenario, a husband and wife are discussing plans for the holidays: Man: "What would you like to do for the holidays?" Woman: "Oh, you can decide, as long as we are together." Man: "How about this year we just do something together?" Woman: "See, I knew you always hated my family." Man: "What? You just said . . . " Woman: "I know what I just said, and you just told me you hate my family" (this of course has no parallel to my own life). What is occurring here is not so much dialogue as people talking at, near, or around each other. Dialogue, as we tend to understand it, implies a back-and-forth interchange between people who are offering, receiving, responding to, and hopefully understanding one another. This is often not the case even in the most basic of everyday interchanges, let alone when communication crosses cultural boundaries.

When we are discussing the possibility of intercultural dialogue, the first thing that we have to confront is whether it is even possible for us to understand people from other cultures at all. To use a fancy academic term from the realm of philosophy of science (because all of those years of graduate school had to be good for something other than keeping me from getting a real job) this is the problem of incommensurability. The basic idea is that each culture represents a distinct theory, paradigm, language game, life world (or whichever fun label you prefer), and because of this there is no common ground or point of comparison from which to even begin the conversation. It would be as if you grew up in a place where everything was blue, people flew, and everything they said was true, and I grew up in place where everything was green, the houses all lean, and people are mean (I am starting to think that I should write the rest of the book in rhyme; I am just not sure whether I will have the time, but I suppose it will be fine). If you accept the idea of incommensurability, these two worlds are so fundamentally different that it is not clear how we could even begin a meaningful dialogue. While there is no doubt that dialogue can be a challenge, the problem with this position is that, as we have noted at various points throughout this book, cultures are dynamic and changing not static and bounded.

Even if we do not accept that cultures are incommensurable and that intercultural dialogue is a real possibility, we are still faced with significant challenges. It is sort of like realizing that it is possible to climb Mount Everest; it is all well and good, but it does not make it easy (although the idea of a having a personal Sherpa is somewhat appealing since I live on the fourth floor of a walk-up building). As we saw in the chapters on China and India, we are at variance with these two cultures on everything from the nature of time and the primacy of the individual or community to the use of squat toilets and toilet paper or absence thereof (something that apparently should not be the topic of class discussion when the director of admissions for the school is observing your class—lets just say she was less than amused). Toilet-paper issue withstanding, questions of time, space, personhood, morality, and the sacred—the stuff of culture—fundamentally alters our encounter and understanding of the world. Because of this, intercultural dialogue, and communication in general, will never be a simple thing. But being that conflict and independence are not really viable options, dialogue is probably the best. Maybe one day we will either succeed in getting rid of everyone who is not like us (terrifying) or learn to sing in perfect harmony (almost equally terrifying), but today is just not that day. In fact, I would like to suggest (and I can because I am the author) that while understanding may be the goal, there is much to be said for misunderstanding—at least at first.

In Praise of Misunderstanding

Misunderstanding is a much-maligned state—it is sort of like New Jersey. But much like New Jersey, once you get past the oil refineries, trash heaps, ghettos, continuous traffic, strange-smelling air, and corrupt politicians, it has much to offer (I would like to point out that much of New Jersey is a charming place with lush forests, farmland, and considerable natural beauty, except the Jersey shore, which even Dante could not have imagined when he was writing Inferno). To be in a state of misunderstanding and be aware that you are in this state is to open yourself up not only to a better understanding of whoever you are in dialogue with, but also yourself. In order to clarify the misunder-standing we not only have to gain awareness of the other but also of ourselves, a point we will return to in a moment. For the most part, whether in our daily lives or when coming into contact with other cultures we interpret them through our own perspective or culture, something that we saw as in both chapters where we looked at the examples of television programming (see how nicely this all fits together). When we become aware of our misunderstanding, for example, talking to people from other cultures about *The OC*, we are presented with an opportunity to arrive at a richer encounter of one another. But before we get to the discussion of how television is the messianic figure that will bring us all together (insert Beatles' song here: "Come together right now, over me"), we have one more point to look at in terms of dialogue and misunderstanding.

Something that we tend not to realize is that we, for the most part, not only misunderstand other cultures, but our own as well (for once I am not just making fun of Americans here; this goes for all cultures—we just happen to be particularly good at misunderstanding). To paraphrase Heidegger, one of my favorite wacky German philosophers (and they all are a curious bunch), we are initially thrown into a world not of our making. What he means by this is that we grow up in a given cultural background, but because it is all we know, we live it and do not necessarily reflect on it. I know that when I stand in line I should give the person in front of me a 2–3-foot cushion of space (which every once in a while I slowly impinge upon just to watch them grow ever more uncomfortable) but I do not know why I do this. I shake hands with people, but do not know how this came to be our primary form of greeting (in an age of antibiotic-resistant bacteria, it might be a good idea to take up the Japanese model of bowing). I live in a 24-hour day, 365-day year, as part of a calendar dated to the early twenty-first century, but seldom do I think about that this is based upon a Western scientific model of astronomy combined with a misdated calculation on the birth of some guy named Jesus (the historical figure Jesus was most likely born around 3 BCE—but hey what is a few years here or there when dating the birth of the son of god). All of this is to say that while we may be the living embodiments of our culture, as scary as that may be, we have very limited reflective awareness of the meaning or origin of how and why we live the way we do and believe what we believe.

If the beginning point for dialogue and communication with other cultures is our own, and we do not have a particularly good understanding of our own culture, it seems fairly unlikely that the dialogue is going to get very far (which of course is not terribly helpful). To go back to the toilet-paper issue for a moment (I hope the admissions director is reading this book—I will have to get her an autographed copy) when I tell my students about how toilet paper is uncommon in certain parts of India and that the left hand is reserved for personal hygiene the response I receive is usually "Ew, I mean ew, that's just like so ew" (they are not always the most articulate group). When I ask them why they think it is any better to wipe their bums with a wad of paper the response is, "Um, well, because, I mean, you know" (ah, the poetry of language). My students do not know why they find the Indian standard less than appealing any more than they know why they find what they do acceptable, because they, like everyone else, live their cultural world without spending much time reflecting on it. If, however, we want to move from misunderstanding to understanding in an intercultural context we are going to need to do something that we the citizens of this great nation of peacemakers and war mongers (you have to love the irony that the country with the largest military spending also has the greatest number of Nobel peace prize winners) are not big fans of self-reflection.

Let's Get Together

Once again, we are going to turn to a rather unlikely source to help us envision a way to deal with intercultural communication and misunderstanding. Rather than looking at communication theory, language theory, or even cultural studies, we are going to instead get our inspiration from a Canadian philosopher (yeah, they actually have things other than hockey players and lumber jacks up there—shocking). While his more recent works have focused on issues of religion, identity, and modernity,[5] Charles Taylor's earlier work focused on issues of philosophy of language and the social sciences. In an essay entitled "Understanding and Ethnocentricity," he suggests that in order to overcome the problem of misunderstanding between cultures we need to arrive at what he terms (in an unnecessarily confusing way—but then he is a philosopher) a "language of perspicuous contact."[6] What he means by this cryptic phrase is that if we are truly going to engage in dialogue and communication in a meaningful way, it cannot be in terms of our cultural metaphors or life world or theirs, it has to be a meeting of the two. It would be like going into Dairy Queen together (I am actually lactose intolerant, so this would be a terrible thing) and trying to decide on something to share. I always get chocolate and you always get vanilla, but rather than one of us trying to convince the other of the virtue of the other flavor, we instead get a chocolate and vanilla swirl (sorry, I am a bit tired, it's the best metaphor I have right now). For us to arrive at a language of perspicuous contact, the first thing that we have to do is move from being a living embodiment of our cultural background, to being consciously aware of the sources and background of our culture. The problem here (besides the fact that it sounds like a whole lot of effort, and we are not really big on effort) is that, as we discussed in Chapters 1 and 2, culture and identity are inexorably intertwined. Because who we are is tied up with our cultural background, it can be more difficult to see beyond our cultural metaphors than it would be to convince the supreme leader of Iran to celebrate holocaust remembrance day. Unlike Ayatollah Khamenei, who is willfully blind to the world around him, we have the capacity to look at ourselves and our culture form a critical perspective. This capacity for self-awareness and self-criticism, although exercised less frequently than those other great American virtues of temperance, moderation, and simplicity (unless of course we think of simplicity as simple mindedness, and then Rush Limbaugh, *Fox News*, Paris Hilton, Anne Coulter, the creators of *Are You Smarter than a Fifth Grader*, reality-TV contestants, and pretty much anyone who likes Oprah would qualify), does open a space in which we can move from living our culture to thinking about and understanding it. Once we have reached this point, then meaningful intercultural communication becomes a real possibility.

Assuming that our interlocutor (an unnecessarily fancy yet fun-to-use word that simply means conversation partner) is as self-aware as we are about the origins and meaning of their cultural sources and what they mean for their self-understanding, when we come together we can begin to discuss not only what we see but also why we see what we do the way that we do, what it means to us, and how it differs from the meaning for the other person. In the process of this conversation, not only does our own self-understanding continue to grow, but so too does our knowledge, understanding, and appreciation of the other (sort of a Barney moment). An experience I had in North India serves as a good example.

I was in the city of Haridwar during the height of the pilgrim season (only in India would there even be a pilgrim season). The temperature was around 115 degrees as I entered the unairconditioned train station so filled with humanity that it made times square look like the Australian outback. After standing in what can best be described as a flood of humanity for well over an hour, I finally reached the ticket window only to be informed, with a big smile and a wobble of the head, that there are no trains. As you might imagine my initial response was a mix of despair, rage, frustration, despondency, confusion, and just a touch of absurdist amusement (it had a nice Beckett sort of feel). When I later discussed this experience with an Indian friend, the response was of course, what did you expect. I expected trains to run somewhat efficiently and on time. I expected to be able to book my tickets online. I expected the unintentional 70s retro kitsch of Amtrak. What I got was a smile, head wobble, and a 7-hour cramped bus ride. Talking over this experience did, however, lead to a broader conversation about my/the Western conception of time and the Eastern conception of time and how my expectation of orderliness is conditioned by a Judeo-Christian worldview that has no parallel in Hinduism. In short, this experience became a point from which a meaningful form of intercultural communication occurred. Unfortunately (or after hearing about that experience many of you may well think quite fortunately) many people do not have the opportunity to have this type of experience first hand. This is why we need the glowing messiah: TV.

The Glowing Messiah

If we are to engage in acts of intercultural communication, we need something to communicate about (profound, I know). Television perhaps better than any other form of media provides us with that something. As we have discussed throughout the book, all cultural products, once they go beyond the boundaries of their original culture, become multivocal and are open to reinterpretation. Television is particularly powerful in this sense because it is a rich source of imagery (and commercials for every conceivable kind of exercise equipment—I am personally fond of combination treadmill stair climber because of how absurdly dangerous it seems) that can be encountered in limitless ways as distinct cultures project their own metaphors onto the programs. There is no doubt that magazines, movies, and the Internet all offer similar opportunities for cultural misunderstanding and dialogue, but magazines are not dynamic, movies are not as continually present, and the Internet is so vast that there is no common ground. In the end, television is particularly useful because it is so ubiquitous (another great but unnecessary word), readily available, continuously changing, and shared in common. There is a wonderful moment of vindication here for all of you who were told by your parents that watching TV was a waste of time—now you can go back to them and inform them with an air of righteous indignation that they were stifling you from pursuing significant intercultural research as a child.

To suggest that television is the perfect medium for use in fostering intercultural dialogue and communication does not mean that it will necessarily be simple to do so. Just because my addiction to *Lost*, which may require me to enter an in-patient treatment program (maybe they can wean me off the show using other less addictive shows—sort of like TV methadone), is shared by someone in China, it does not mean that he or she and I are going to reverse a half century of cultural misunderstanding between the great imperial power and the middle kingdom (although both of our countries do also love KFC so we have that going for us—who knows, maybe all we need is Season 1 of *Lost* and a bucket of chicken to bring about world peace). What it does mean is that, given the opportunity, American television programming can serve as a great meeting point between cultures that allows for a space of communication of shared images and yet distinct interpretation based upon a range of cultural inheritances and metaphors. To clarify how and why we understand the images the way we do is to foster a deep understanding of the other, as well as more complex and nuanced understanding of ourselves.

This book, other than serving as a forum for my meandering train of thought and pointless musings, has been an attempt to clarify the interrelation between television, culture, identity, and communication, so as to move us toward a better understanding of how these things fit together in a complex, dynamic, war-filled, conflict-ridden, yet wonderful and bizarre, Disney-loving, Coca Cola–drinking, McDonald's-eating global world. While we specifically looked at American television programs in China and India, the same idea holds for anywhere that American television is found. As long as the glowing messiah is sending out multivocal programs that are being encountered by diverse audiences, we will have something to talk about and a starting point for meaningful intercultural communication—God help us all.

Notes

1. Martin, Judith N., and Thomas K. Nakayama. *Intercultural Communication in Contexts.* 5th ed. McGraw Hill Higher Education, 2009.
2. Samovar, Larry A., Richard E. Porter, and Edwin R. McDaniel. *Intercultural Communication: A Reader.* 12th ed. Wadsworth Publishing, 2008.
3. Ting-Toomey, Dr. Stella W.C., and Felipe Korzenny. *Language, Communication, and Culture: Current Directions.* Sage Publications, Inc., 1989.
4. Barbour, Ian G. *Religion and Science.* Rev Sub. HarperOne, 1997.
5. Taylor, Charles. *A Secular Age.* Belknap Press of Harvard University Press, 2007.
6. Taylor, Charles. *Philosophical Papers: Vol. 2: Philosophy and the Human Sciences.* Cambridge University Press, 1985.

Suggestions for Further Reading

Allen, Brenda J. *Difference Matters: Communicating Social Identity.* Waveland Press, Inc., 2003.

Barbour, Ian G. *Religion and Science.* Rev Sub. HarperOne, 1997.

Bernstein, Richard J. *Beyond Objectivism and Relativism: Science, Hermeneutics, and Praxis.* University of Pennsylvania Press, 1983.

Habermas, Jürgen. *Lifeworld and System: A Critique of Functionalist Reason.* Beacon Press, 1985.

Korzenny, Felipe, Dr. Stella W. C. Ting-Toomey, and Elizabeth Schiff. *Mass Media Effects across Cultures.* Sage Publications, Inc., 1992.

Martin, Judith N., and Thomas K. Nakayama. *Intercultural Communication in Contexts.* 5th ed. McGraw Hill Higher Education, 2009.

Samovar, Larry A., Richard E. Porter, and Edwin R. McDaniel. *Intercultural Communication: A Reader.* 12th ed. Wadsworth Publishing, 2008.

Schutz, Alfred, and Thomas Luckmann. *Structures of the Life-World,* Vol. 1. 1st ed. Northwestern University Press, 1973.

Taylor, Charles. *A Secular Age.* Belknap Press of Harvard University Press, 2007.

—. *Philosophical Papers: Vol. 2: Philosophy and the Human Sciences.* Cambridge University Press, 1985.

Ting-Toomey, Dr. Stella W. C., and Felipe Korzenny. *Language, Communication, and Culture: Current Directions.* Sage Publications, Inc., 1989.

Conclusion

Scene #2: China

As I am lying in bed in my questionable hotel in Shanghai that I have grown ever more convinced is simply the front for a brothel, my cell phone rings. The voice on the other end of the line that is trembling from both excitement and fear from having to speak in English, informs me that my flight scheduled for tomorrow to Jinan has been canceled. After my initial sense of relief, being that the idea of having to fly on a Chinese airline is somewhat more troubling than the fact that people actually take Oprah seriously; the now somewhat more confident young woman informs me that there is another plane that will take me there. When I inquire about the airline she informs me to go to the airport, at which point she just hangs up. Not knowing which airport, terminal, airline, or time, I decide to role the dice and show up around when my original flight was scheduled.

Upon arriving at the airport I go to the ticket counter of the airline on which I was originally scheduled, which to me seems a logical choice, but I have clearly forgotten that Western logic does not apply in China. After standing in something that was somewhere between a line and a mob, with people who seemed to be competing with each other to see who could yell the loudest at their accompanying family members (I have none with me, so I sadly cannot participate in the fun), I finally reach a representative who upon seeing me immediately directs me to someone else. After about half an hour or so of similar lines and inter- actions, and a bit of yelling of my own since everyone else was doing it and I do not have much to do while I wait, I finally reach someone who seemed willing to help. My attempt to explain my situation probably makes about as much sense as an evangelical Southern preacher at a prochoice rally, but in the end the oddly amiable fellow prints out a piece of paper and points toward the security gates. At this point I am so confused and disoriented that I decided not to question it. By some act of Buddha, Confucius, or the imaginary Lao-Tzu I actually ended up on a plane . . . to the right destination.

After about an hour and a half of continuous prayers to Guanyin (the bodhisattva of compassion) I safely land in Jinan, a small (by Chinese standards) industrial city located about half way between Beijing and Shanghai. As much as I would like this to be my final destination, I unfortunately still have miles to go before I sleep, as I am heading for Taishan—the holiest mountain in China. Having claimed my bag, I enter into the arrivals hall to find, much to my surprise, a desk that says visitors information in English. Delighted with this bit of luck I walk up to the desk with my confident American swagger, smile, and ask very politely where I might find the bus to Taishan. The young woman behind the desk looks at me, pauses, and then as if I was not even there, walks away. With every attempt to communicate comes a similar response to the point where I finally look in a mirror to make sure I am here and had not actually died on the plane ride and entered some type of Sartian vision of hell or perhaps a Chinese version of Waiting for Godot. Realizing the absurdist amusement and yet ultimate futility of my attempt to get help, I decide to just hire a cab. I will spare you the details of the initial encounter with the cab driver, but assure you that it goes so poorly that he drives me to the wrong place, grossly overcharges me, and spends the entire hour ride pointing at me and laughing hysterically—I love China.

My cab driver, who is clearly competing to win the Ms. Congeniality prize, refuses to drive me anywhere but the bus station in Jinan. Being that painfully polluted industrial cities do not make it high on the tourism list, I am fairly sure that I am the only Westerner to have entered this bus station—ever. With just about every set of eyes staring at me as though the abominable snowman just showed up at an all-inclusive Caribbean resort, I find the one person in the entire station with whom I can communicate. I lay a 500 Yuan note on the counter, since I cannot hear the price through the yelling crowds (yelling is apparently quite big in China), get a ticket that I cannot read, and am pointed toward a gate whose number I cannot decipher. Arriving at the gate I hand my ticket to a man in a uniform, maybe a bus attendant, maybe a police officer, maybe a janitor, maybe a guy who just likes dressing up, but at this point I am not terribly concerned. He stares at me, stares at the ticket, stares at me, stares at the ticket, stares at me, then takes a long hard look at the ticket, takes an even longer look at me, and then as though in some epiphany in which he realizes where he is, points for me to get on the bus. Not that I am a particularly tall person, but Chinese busses were apparently built by smurfs, and I spend the next 2 hours with my knees in my chest sitting next to one woman who is carrying a baby that is not wearing a diaper (I cannot imagine how this is going to end well) and another who seems so absolutely terrified of me that if she presses herself any more closely to the window I am afraid she might fall out.

Arriving in Taishan, without being urinated on or having the woman next to me have a heart attack, I count myself fairly lucky until of course I step off the bus to find that it seems as though my cab driver had called ahead since everyone in the bus depot begins, as if on cue, to point and laugh at me. Beginning to feel a bit self-conscious, I decide to go find my hotel where I encounter the sign, "Welcome customers with smile from all : over the world." While I have no idea what this means, why there is a word with an ampersand in the middle, and if it is them or me that is required to have the smile I decide to check in anyway. After being told 7 different prices for 23 different types of rooms, the main difference being the use of the words deluxe, superior, ultra, and special in randomly selected order, I decide to opt for the special, deluxe, ultra superior room, which upon entering I quickly come to realize deserves none of those modifiers. Nor does the restaurant, which serves me a meal entitled vegetable heaven that consists of tofu skins filled with vegetables that taste like they were soaked in formaldehyde, floating in what can only be described as brown Jell-O. Perhaps whoever translated the title interchanged the words heaven and death. I think I should just try again tomorrow.

With the rising of the morning light I prepare myself for the days spiritual journey up the sacred mountain. I do a bit of meditation, a bit of tai chi, say some prayers (might as well cover all of my bases), and

leave for the sacred Taoist temple dedicated to the goddess of the mountain. I enter hundreds of year old structure with due reverence and
solemnity. Approaching the main altar I purchase incense to make an
offering, and slowly walk up to pay my respects. Just as I light the incense
and begin the sequence of bowing and prostration I hear a voice punc-
ture the calm. "American! American! American! Please, please take a
picture with you." A boy of about 13 comes running up to me dressed
head to toes in Nike clothing with his parents close behind. This friendly
if insistent young man proceeds to take numerous pictures with me
standing in front of what is suppose to be one of the holiest Taoist shrines
with me holding my incense in one hand while he makes a peace sign.
As he walks away he yells back, "I love USA," while I am left with a line
from the Tao Te Ching echoing in my head, "If you realize that all things
change, there is nothing you will try to hold on to."

   The reason I begin the ending (this is either ironic or an oxymoron—
I cannot quite decide which) with this scene is that it embodies much
of what we have been discussing throughout the book—the strong
interrelation between identity, culture, and media in a global age and
how that in turn impacts intercultural communication. In some ways the
topics in this book have been fairly far ranging, yet like the ingredients
of a cake before they are baked all are distinct entities with no direct
relationship; once put together they form a warm, delicious, satisfying,
artery-clogging, diabetes-inducing, obesity-causing goodness (unlike a
cake, however; the elements of this book should have had no negative
health effects, except mental, but that's not covered by insurance, so it
does not count). In large measure, each of the chapters have been in
the service of how we can go about understanding who and what we are
in an ever-more complex, interrelated, dynamic, fast-paced, media-
saturated world.
   As was stated in the introduction, China and India were strategically
chosen for this work for a few reasons. The primary reason was of course
the food, which after having traveled through China I quickly realized
was not particularly sound reasoning (while I enjoy peanut oil as much
as the next person, I felt so greasy after most of my meals that I could
have used a slip-and-slide without water). While the food in India did
make up for its neighbor north of the Himalayas (and Tibetan plateau),

there are better reasons to choose these two Asian powerhouses than their cuisines—namely, the fact that they are Asian powerhouses (as you well know by now, I am a master of the obvious).

If you are able to pull yourselves away from *Gossip Girl*, *The Biggest Loser*, and *Dancing with the Stars* long enough to turn on CNN, MSNBC, or even Fox News, which is usually more entertaining and fictional than anything else on TV anyway, you cannot go more than a few minutes without hearing some story about the recentering of world power, the rise of China, the new economic powerhouse of the Asian economies, or the derailment on an Indian train (which does seem to occur with a disturbing frequency, but is a risk I am willing to take to get 20-cent cups of oh so sweet, milky, and delicious chai served out of gigantic metal containers that probably have not been cleaned since the last age of Vishnu). One thing all of these stories have in common is a particular kind of uniquely American fatalism (remember our sense of the ever-impending apocalypse), which predicts the downfall, end, destruction, or collapse of the American century, dominance, world, or empire. In the midst of all of this harbingers of doom no attention is paid to the actual cultures, backgrounds, or people of the countries that are supposedly going to replace us.

On the other side of the spectrum from the ever so entertaining yet equally uninformative cable news stations, we have an army of academics (not that they could actually form an army since they would spend far too much time having seminars, colloquiums, and committee meetings about the meaning, purpose, ethical implications, leadership style, global implications, theoretical problems, and methodological inconsistencies of the effort) portending the end of cultural diversity through the rise of American cultural hegemony. In other words, us White folks have found new ways to oppress the poor through media instead of armies (not that we don't still enjoy a good, old-fashioned war every once in a while). Much like their cable news counterparts, those who study globalization, culture, and identity spend so much time talking about an idea that they tend to forget to actually look and see what is going on. Perhaps they take the words of Marcus Aurelius a bit too seriously, "Our life is what our thoughts make it."

In this book, we have attempted to look at China and India in order to focus on how the interaction between globalization, identity, and culture is actually being played out through television. In the end, what we have come to see is that American culture is in no way supplanting, replacing, or otherwise co-opting Chinese or Indian culture. Rather, what Chinese and Indian audiences encounter when they watch American television programming is, wait for it, wait for it, wait for it, themselves. As we have seen, once cultural products, television or otherwise, leave their cultures of origin they become multivocal and open to the reinterpretation and projection of the cultural metaphors of the cultures in which they find themselves. This is to say that *Prison Break* in china is about China and not about America (they can have the third season anyway, since it wasn't very good—stupid writers strike).

While the analysis we have pursued throughout the book has been specifically directed at China and India, a similar approach could be taken for any other culture. Whether we turn to the school girl–obsessed, sadistic game show–watching, hyper-modern, pop culture wonderland of Japan, or the vodka-soaked, borscht-eating, totalitarian tendencies of Russia, or the burka-wearing, antimodern, party animals in Afghanistan, we can pursue a similar approach. The goal is to illuminate the unique cultural metaphors, inheritances, background, or lifeworld (or whatever descriptor you desire to insert after the word cultural—I also like milieu, ethos, norms, baggage, furniture . . .) so as to open a space of encounter and understanding that neither gives way to conflict or simple accep-tance (as much as I like the idea of the world being one big happy Coke commercial) but rather meaningful dialogue.

I am not going to sit here and tell you that dialogue is easy (well, actually I am going to sit here, since I am a bit tired from all of this writing and sort of need a nap, but I still won't tell you that dialogue is easy). For us to successfully communicate across cultural boundaries, we first need to understand the relationship between our own culture and identity (something not terribly common in this great land of Evangelical Christian theme parks; Rush Limbaugh; Oprah; E! Enter-tainment Television; people who name their children Madison, Savannah, Montana, or Dakota; gas-guzzling SUVs with American flag stickers; Wife Swap; and people who eat brunch at 4:00—once its past 12, it's just lunch). We also need to have some understanding of the culture with which we are communicating (again unlikely in a country in which only 27% of its citizens have passports, and in which there are students who, when about to go on a trip to Japan, express their excitement because they love Chinese food—true story). This is certainly not likely, but nor is it impossible.

Perhaps in the end, if we are going to move toward meaningful intercultural communication in our rapidly changing world, we have no greater asset than the glowing messiah that is television. Sitting in front of its radiating warmth we see ourselves in all of our KFC-eating, NASCAR-watching, gun-toting, Big Gulp–drinking, Brittney Spears–worshiping, suburban-despairing, Disneyfied, meaningless, consumerist, resplendent glory. But even as we see ourselves as we are, so too are people from other cultures seeing themselves as they are. If we can come and sit together in front of the glowing, irradiating goodness of television and understand how and why we see things the way we do, we may just have a chance of having an interesting conversation. Or at least we can share different kinds of interesting snack foods.

Well, that's it, but stay tuned for the next exciting episode where the brothers from *Prison Break* team up with the people from *Heroes* to help free the survivors on the *Lost* island, and they celebrate by watching a *Simpsons* marathon with the characters from *Friends* . . . or something like that.

Index

America and Americans, distinction
  between 131–2
American culture 48–9
American fatalism 162
American identity
  negative side 128–31
  positive side 127–8
  see also identity
American Idol 38
American psyche 127, 130
As the World Turns 119
Aurelius, Marcus 162

Barbour, Ian 146
Barthes, Roland 40
Bauman, Zygmunt 24–5
Berlin, Isaiah 49
Bhagavad Gita 93
Bodhisattvas 60
Britain 132
Buddha 59, 60, 61, 67
Buddhism 59–61

cable news stations 162
Canada 132
cartoons 112
China 4, 53–5, 132, 134–5, 136, 144,
  158–61, 162
  Buddhism 59–61
  China Central Television 134–5
  Chinese Central Television 69–71
  Communism 64
  Confucianism 55–7
  contemporary culture 66–7
  Friends in 75–8
  government's control on TV 71–4

Internet 72–3
Lost in 82–5
Maoism 62–5
news agencies' portray of
  American 135
Prison Break 79–81
Taoism 57–9
Christianity 66, 81, 91–2
Chuang Tzu 59
circumventor 73
Clinton, Hillary Rodham 109
CNN 107
Colbert, Steven 23
communication
  across cultures 6
  see also intercultural communication
conflict model, of intercultural
  communication 146–8
Confucianism 55–7
Confucius 55–6, 61, 67
cultural studies
  structural versus contextual 47–8
cultures 4, 18–23, 139
  dynamic quality of 20, 23
  interaction between 108
  see also intercultural communication

Dallas 119
Derrida, Jacques 108
Des Moines Register 73
dharma (duty) 92–3, 94, 96, 113
dialogue model, intercultural
  communication 149–51
dominant decoding, of media
  message 42
Doordarshan 106

165